Round the World with Bicycles

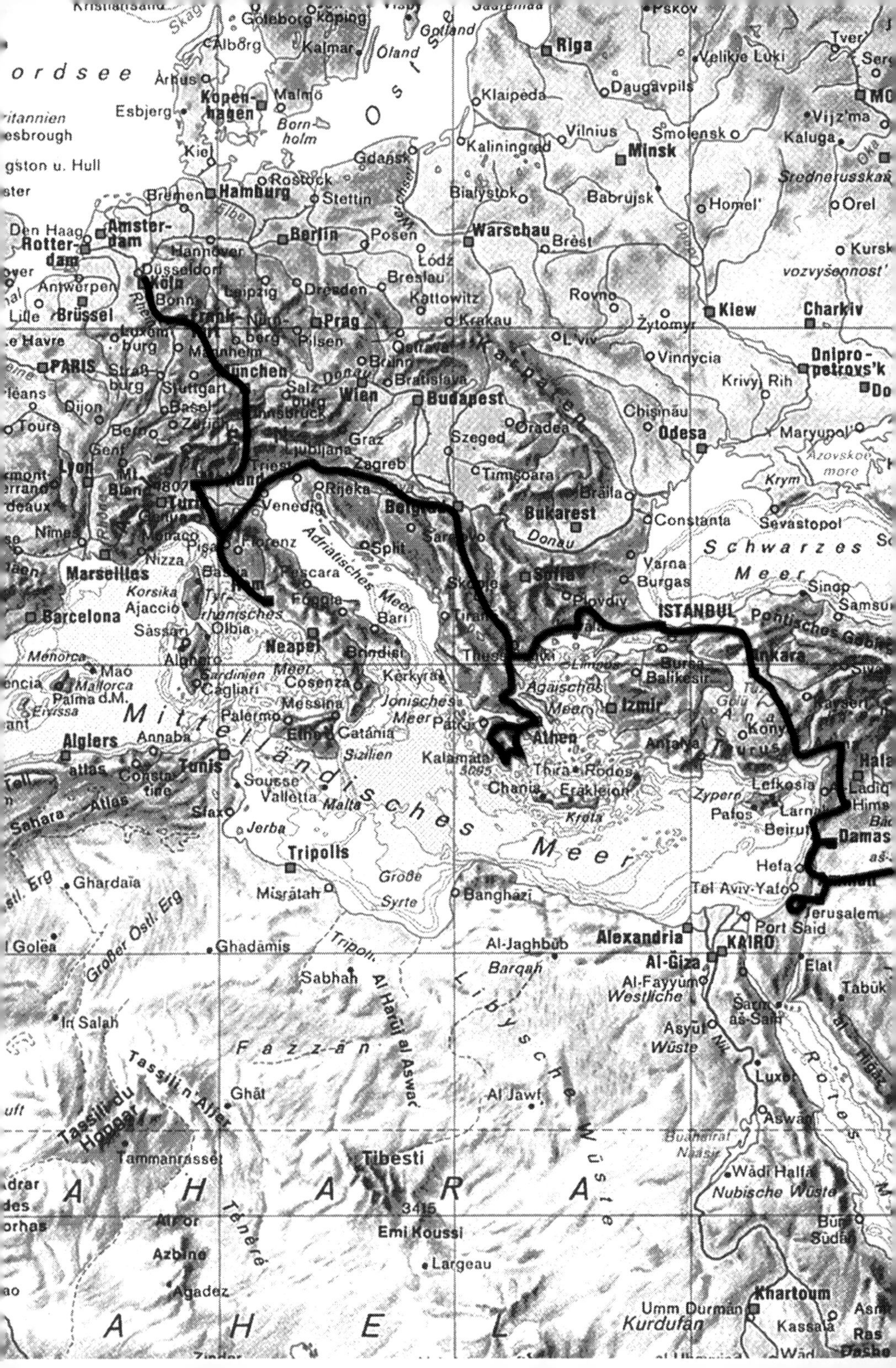

Göteborg
Kalmar
Öland
Gotland
Riga
Pskov
Velikie Luki
Ålborg
Nordsee
Århus
Kopenhagen
Malmö
Bornholm
Esbjerg
Ostsee
Klaipeda
Daugavpils
Vilnius
Smolensk
Vjaz'ma
Kaluga
Kiel
Gdansk
Kaliningrad
Minsk
Rostock
Bremen
Hamburg
Stettin
Bialystok
Babrujsk
Homel'
Orel
Den Haag
Amsterdam
Rotterdam
Berlin
Posen
Warschau
Brest
Kursk
Hannover
Lodz
Düsseldorf
Antwerpen
Köln
Leipzig
Dresden
Breslau
Bonn
Kattowitz
Rovno
Lille
Brüssel
Prag
Krakau
Kiew
Charkiv
Le Havre
Luxemburg
Nürnberg
Pilsen
Zytomyr
Mannheim
Ostrava
L'viv
PARIS
Straßburg
München
Brünn
Vinnycia
Dnipropetrovs'k
Stuttgart
Salzburg
Wien
Bratislava
Budapest
Krivyj Rih
Dijon
Basel
Innsbruck
Tours
Bern
Zürich
Chisinau
Odesa
Maryupol'
Genf
Graz
Szeged
Oradea
Lyon
Triest
Ljubljana
Zagreb
Timisoara
Mt. Blanc
Rijeka
Braila
Krym
Venedig
Turin
Belgrad
Bukarest
Nîmes
Monaco
Florenz
Split
Sarajevo
Donau
Constanta
Sevastopol
Nizza
Pisa
Schwarzes Meer
Marseilles
Bastia
Rom
Pescara
Adriatisches Meer
Sofia
Varna
Burgas
Korsika
Ajaccio
Foggia
Skopje
Plovdiy
Sinop
Barcelona
Olbia
Bari
Tirana
ISTANBUL
Pontisches Gebirge
Sassari
Neapel
Brindisi
Thessaloniki
Bursa
Ankara
Menorca
Alghero
Sardinien
Kerkyra
Balikesir
Mao
Mallorca
Cagliari
Cosenza
Ägäisches Meer
Palma d.M.
Messina
Jonisches Meer
Izmir
Eivissa
Mittelländisches Meer
Palermo
Patras
Athen
Algiers
Annaba
Etna
Catania
Antalya
Konya
Sizilien
Kalamata
Taurus
Tunis
Constantine
Thira
Rodos
Lefkosia
Sousse
Chania
Eraklejon
Zypern
Valletta
Malta
Kreta
Pafos
Beirut
Sahara-Atlas
Sfax
Damas
Jerba
Tripolis
Meer
Hefa
Ghardaia
Große Syrte
Misratah
Banghazi
Tel Aviv-Yafo
Jerusalem
Großer Östl. Erg
Port Said
El Golea
Ghadamis
Al-Jaghbub
Alexandria
KAIRO
Al-Giza
Sabhah
Barqah
Elat
Al-Fayyum
Westliche
Libysche Wüste
Tabuk
In Salah
Al Haruj al Aswad
Fazzan
Asyut
Wüste
Nil
Tassili n'Ajjer
Ghat
Al Jawf
Luxor
Rotes Meer
Tassili du Hoggar
Aswan
Tammanrasset
Tibesti
Buhairat Nasir
Wadi Halfa
Nubische Wüste
SAHARA
Ténéré
3415
Emi Koussi
Air
Azbine
Largeau
Agadez
Khartoum
Umm Durman
SAHEL
Kurdufan
Kassala

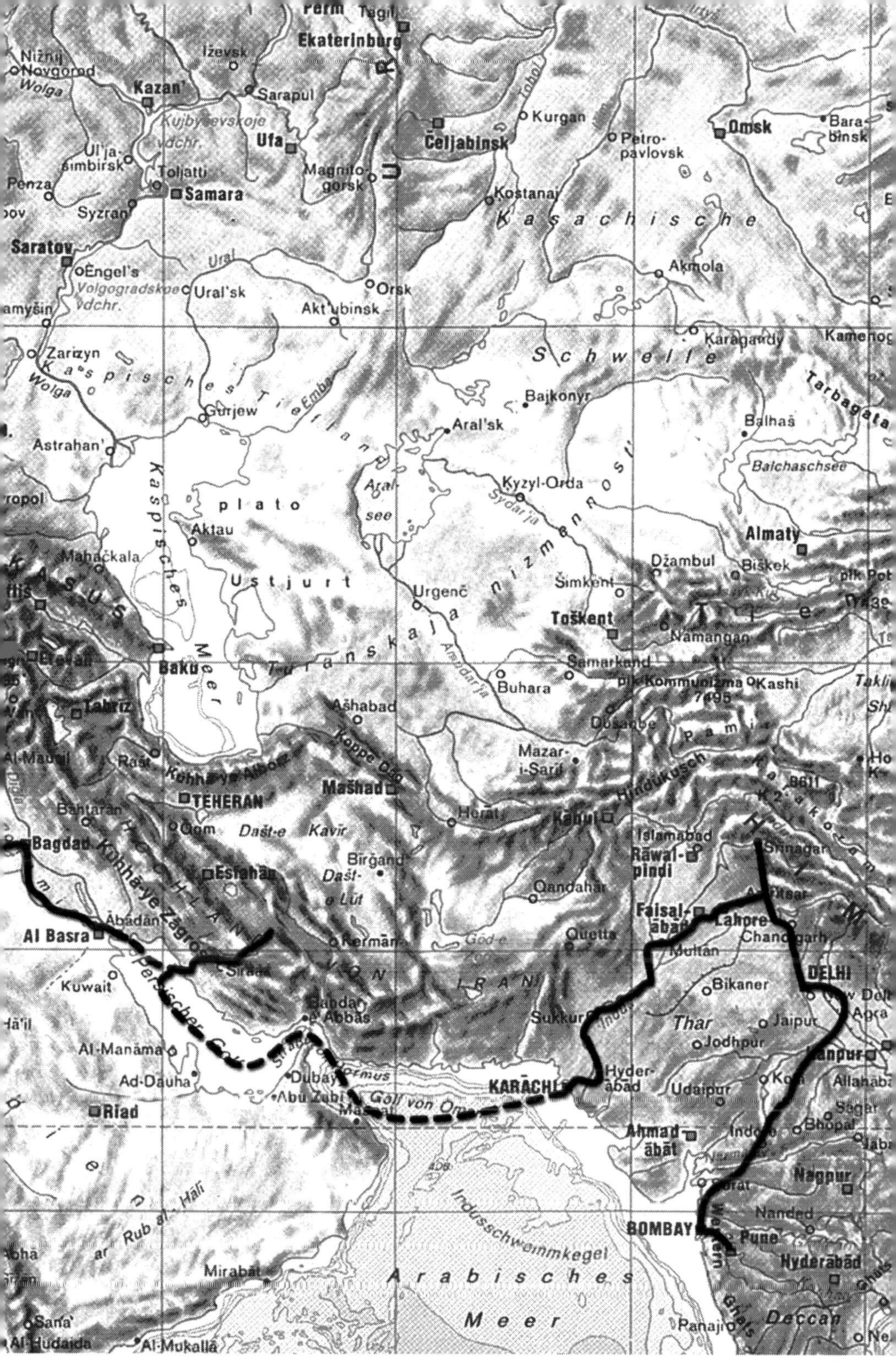
Perm
Tagil
Ekaterinburg
Nižnij Novgorod
Wolga
Iževsk
Kazan'
Sarapul
Kujbyševskoje vdchr.
Tobol
Kurgan
Omsk
Barabinsk
Ufa
Čeljabinsk
Petropavlovsk
Ul'janovsk
Toljatti
Magnitogorsk
Penza
Samara
Syzran'
Kostanaj
Kasachische
Saratov
Engel's
Volgogradskoe vdchr.
Ural
Ural'sk
Orsk
Akmola
Kamyšin
Akt'ubinsk
Karaganda
Zarizyn
Kaspisches Tiefland
Schwelle
Emba
Tarbagatai
Bajkonyr
Gurjew
Aral'sk
Balhaš
Astrahan'
Balchaschsee
Aralsee
Kyzyl-Orda
Sydarja
plato
Stavropol
Almaty
Aktau
Kaspisches Meer
Mahačkala
Džambul
Biškek
Ustjurt
Turanskaja nizmennost'
Šimkent
Urgenč
Taškent
Namangan
Baku
Amudarja
Samarkand
Buhara
pik Kommunizma 7495
Kashi
Tabriz
Ašhabad
Koppe Dāg
Dušanbe
Pamir
Mazar-i-Šarif
Rašt
Kuhhā-ye Alborz
Hindukusch
TEHERAN
Mašhad
8611 K 2
Karakorum
Qom
Dašt-e Kavir
Herat
Kabul
Bagdad
Islamabad
Rāwalpindi
Srinagar
Birǧand
Esfahān
Dašt-e Lūt
Kuhhā-ye Zagros
Qandahār
Faisalābād
Abādān
Al Basra
Lahore
Kermān
Quetta
Chandigarh
Multān
Kuwait
Persischer Golf
Irān
DELHI
Bikaner
Bandar Abbās
Sukkur
Thar
Jaipur
Indus
Al-Manāma
Jodhpur
Kanpur
Straße von Hormus
Hyderābād
Ad-Dauha
Dubay
KARACHI
Udaipur
Allahabad
Abu Zubi
Golf von Oman
Riad
Masqat
Ahmadābād
Indore
Bhopal
Nagpur
Surat
Rub al Hāli
Indusschwemmkegel
Nanded
BOMBAY
Pune
Mirabat
Hyderābād
Arabisches Meer
Sana'
Al-Hudaida
Al-Mukallā
Panaji
Ghats
Deccan

Om Prakash Virmani
»Round The World With Bicycles«
ISBN 3-8311-2688-7

Originalausgabe
1. Auflage 2002

Konzept Gestaltung und Satz: ad libitum, W. Lesicar, Stuttgart
Umschag: ad libitum, W. Lesicar, Stuttgart
Druck und Bindearbeiten: Book On Demand, Hamburg
Printed in Germany

Prologue

I was born 1930, in Quetta (Pakistan today). I migrated with my parents to India two years before the partition of the country took place in 1947 in an Indian union and Pakistan. I studied at the Engineering College in Poona. The idea to visit Europe and other countries was born during the final year of the studies at the Engineering College in Poona.

The idea to make the journey by bicycles was initiated by my friend and organiser Mr. Ishaq Baluch. It was during the last stage of our preparations for the journey that Sadanand Prabhakar Kotwal, also a graduated engineer joined us as the third Musketeer.

All three of us belonged to well situated families and had the possibility to travel by air or by ship, however, the internal firmness to make the journey by bicycles than by the aforesaid means and with the minimum amount of money to our disposal was a challenge.

It was obvious that an objection by our parents to carry out the journey as planed by us was expected, however, we were firm to accept the challenge and this way convinced our parents.

The main object of our journey was to come to know many people on our route, exchange the views concerning culture, customs and obviously to promote mutual friendships.

On our route we tried, so far possible, to stay at the student hostels of the schools and of universities and this way met many students in each country on our route and had the chance to make many friends.

We thank to the organisation World Wide Brotherhood, who had arranged a grand farewell reception at the Cricket Club of India in Bombay, where the home minister Mr. S. K. Patil presided the reception with many diplomatic and cultural representatives of different countries of Middle East and Europe.

We tried to follow the motto of the WWB throughout our journey and came to know many young students and other cultural representatives.

Remarks of the author:

During my visit to Jerusalem by bycicle in 1955, I could with disperse note the division of the city in an Arabian part and a Jewish one, where in the evenings the lights were put out to avoid the danger of being hurt by the exchanged bullets by the two opponent parties. Now though Jerusalem is no more divided yet it is a cause of dispute and conflict between Palestinians and Israel. I believe that lot of water through Nile shall have flown before Israel and Palestinians live in peace together.

Few months after I came to the divided Germany in different political zones (American, British, French and Russian), I had the opportunity to watch in the German TV the tragic and overwhelming scenes when the prisoners of war from Russia were received by their friends and relatives. I sincerely wished that there are no more wars and that the divided country unites again. This cherished desire was fulfilled in 1989, after the fall of the Berlin wall.

The first five countries founded as European Economic Community (EEC) in 1955 have now consolidated 15 countries as a European Union and there is a great optimistic hope that more European countries shall follow in this movement of consolidation. While writing this book I realised that in the last 40 years many changes have taken place in the countries we had travelled, such as for example no more monarchies exist in Persia and Greece. Also the communist country Yugoslavia has been divided in three different independent states; the West and the East Germany has now united as one country. I greatly hope that in the near future North and South Korea shall follow the way Germany did.

I dedicate this book to my whole family whose incitement and support encouraged me to write down my experiences.

I thank our daughter Indra for her immense help in editing, Walter Lesicar for the concept and design of this book and our son Arun for the reproduction of the photographs.

This book is an obligation to my late friend Ishaq Baluch and his family. Unfortunately Ishaq Baluch, married to Haleema, a charming woman with four lovely children, died on 2nd January 1991 in Montreal (Canada).

Round the World with Bicycles

The Beginning

IT ALL BEGAN DURING THE FINAL YEAR OF OUR GRADUATION. The thesis of our graduation was »Noise measurement on the short and medium wave broadcasting and methods of their reduction«. It was onc of those late evenings in the year 1954 in the labs of the Telecommunication faculty of College of Engineering in Poona, where we were just busy in measuring the values of noise interference on the short wave transmission with the ionosphere possibly at its lower position in the atmosphere.

Our Professor Mr. Aiya who had his residence in the Premises of the college entered the labs and saw us busy with our work. He started a conversation with us about other topics of life than the problems of noise interference. He seemed to be in a joyous mood and began narrating to us about his adventures during his graduation studies in Great Britain and how he had managed to travel round Europe with very less money to his disposal. For example in France he acted as a fortune-teller wearing a Turkish cap to attract the attention of the people and interpreted the lines on their hands and this way made a little contribution to his budget for travel.

Referring to the Indian traditions he remarked that Indian traditions dominate to a greater extent the way of life, for example a young graduate, who is supported financially by his parents is interested to complete the studies as soon as possible and has possibly rare or no chances to see the world before settling down in life.

The facts are that usually the parents of a young Indian start searching for a match for the marriage as soon as he has completed the studies and has secured a job. Professor Aiya encouraged us all to see the world if possible before settling down.

Ishaq and myself were impressed by the idea. One evening when we were strolling on the main street Ishaq came back to comments of our professor and discussed with me about the possibilities of undertaking such a venture. After we had exchanged our views it became apparent that travelling by ship or by air would not be possible because it would require a good amount of money, which we both did not possess at that time. We then kept aside the idea for the time being to be discussed later on with possible alternatives.

One evening Ishaq visited me and was full of excitement and showed me a book, which he had discovered in the city library written by a Parsee (a Zoroastrian descended from Persian refugees settled principally in Bombay) who in 1926 together with five parsees had toured round the world by bicycles with very less amount of money to their disposal.

Ishaq was fascinated from the venture described in the book and asked me about my opinion about it. I personally found the idea a fantastic one, however, considering the aspect that we were students and dependent upon the assistance of our parents was not sure whether I could convince my father, who had to give his consent for such an adventure. Ishaq had to face the same difficulty but had to convince his mother. His father had expired when he was a boy of ten.

Our college was situated about five kilometers from our residence. We covered this distance daily by bicycles. The bicycle was our important conveyance, companion and obviously the important means for the daily provisions and many other similar requirements. Even for the evening stroll on the main street where the motto was »to see and to be seen« we towed the bicycle while walking along the main street. Our bicycle was a great help when we visited the late cinema shows in English because after the show hardly any public conveyance was available.

Whenever we were together in the college or in the circle of our friends we could not avoid discussing about the journey of those Parsees and about our own possibilities. One evening when we were together we met a group of members of World Wide Brotherhood who after hearing about our mission spontaneously declared that if we decided to make the journey by bicycles they shall arrange a grand see off with many representatives of Politics and Industry. We were impressed about the idea. However, the immediate task was to complete the studies, obtain the Graduation in Telecommunication Engineering and thereafter start with the preparations for the journey.

We got together to discuss about the route of the journey, thereby we realised that we shall have to study a lot of literature concerning languages, culture etc. of the countries lying along the route we intended to follow. Also it seemed necessary to study the traditional, cultural and other aspects of our own country to be prepared in any case for the questions that may arise when we would meet people on our route. As such we had very less or in some cases absolutely no knowledge of the way of life maintained by the people living in other parts of India. To obtain the necessary information we visited the government tourist offices and collected the literature and borrowed books from the city library over all the states of our country. Also we made it a point to meet people who had been abroad and could provide us with information regarding the regulations valid in each country and tips how we could master the difficulties.

During this preparation time I remember to have mentioned to my father about our conversation with our professor and that we should go abroad to gain more experiences in our subject of studies with the intention to know his reflections, however, not disclosing to him that such a journey by bicycles was a possibility. He did not seem to sympathise with the idea and meant that we had also chances to work and gain experiences in India, too.

Preparations

At last it was in March 1954 when we were handed over our graduation certificates. Now the preparations for the journey could be started. The first task was to secure a passport. The formalities for getting a passport were very strict. It was only seven years after India had obtained its independence. Mr. Jawaharlal Nehru was the Prime Minister of India. The country was trying hard to meet the new situation. There were lots of restrictions imposed for the export of hard currency. Any Indian going abroad was reminded that he is like a representative of the country and should try to represent the country adequately. Furthermore a guarantor was to be provided, in case of repatriation when the person had to face difficulties abroad. From the conversation with my father I knew that he would not agree to my venture. I was expecting an opposition and a lot of difficulties for obtaining a passport.

Ishaqs grandfather had studied Architecture in Great Britain and knew quite well about the formalities to be fulfilled for travelling abroad. After knowing about my difficulties he declared to give a guarantee for me in case my father would refuse to give one. Both Ishaq and myself filled in the forms for passports and sent these to the passport authorities in Bombay. Just at this stage of preparations another fellow student Mr. Sadanand Prabhakar Kotwal (his nick name was Nana) showed interest for our plans and wished to join us. We had the motto »the more the merrier«. Now we were three for the world tour. Nana started preparing for the journey too. For the application of the passport we had to declare the countries we wished to visit and the amount of the hard currency in form of bank notes or in form of travelling cheques we intended to carry so that correct entrance could be made in the passport. I had earned about 800 Rupees during the college holidays, this money was equivalent to 59 English Pounds. I applied for travelling cheques by »Thos. Cook & Sons«

in Bombay for this amount. Ishaq and Nana each had about the same amount to spend for the journey.

I was not at home, when the registered letter from the passport authorities arrived. I believe it was a lucky moment for me that my father received it for me. When I came home and saw the sad face of my father, I asked him whether anything had happened, he handed over the envelope to me with the comment »Well it seems that you have made it«. He sincerely wished that I reconsidered my plans and should not undertake the journey by bicycle and declared seriously to help me financially or otherwise and proposed to make the journey by ship or by plane rather than the said hard way.

It was difficult for me to convince my father that it was worth travelling by road and by bicycles. Next day when Ishaq visited me and then we both did our best to convince my father with arguments and promises to inform him about all the details when we had worked these out. I believe he understood that we should have such a chance and allowed me to carry on with the necessary preparations.

At first we had a plan to apply for the visas for Pakistan, Iran, Iraq, but then we decided to get the visa for Pakistan only. The remaining visas should be obtained in Lahore or Karachi depending upon the route we shall be allowed to take in Pakistan.

Somebody from the circle of our friends mentioned that an international Association by the name "World Wide Brotherhood" existed and we should contact them. The members of the said association in Poona invited us. We had a long discussion and exchange of views and this way gained more insight of their activities. After knowing their motives, we decided to make the motto of this association as our motto for the journey. The members in Poona informed their associate friends in Bombay so that they could develop further activities to make our journey more public.

We had to secure the necessary items, like sleeping bags, bags for the bicycles and other necessities. Someone from our circle of friends told us to make a trip to the biggest second-hand market in Bombay, where the possibility to get the said items was much greater than in Poona. I was in possession of a bicycle which had no gear-change-mechanism, so I was hopeful to secure a bicycle with such mechanism at this market. We all three travelled by train to Bombay and visited the market. Luckily I could buy an English bicycle (Trade Mark Raleigh) with three speed gear system. Also we could get the side bags for the bicycle. We could not, however, get the necessary sleeping bags. Someone indicated to us about the possibility of obtaining the sleeping bags if we knew someone in the army. Our class mate Mr. Avtar Singh Oberoi declared that he would consult his father who was officer in the army, whether he could arrange the sleeping bags for at least two of us. Ishaq and myself were grateful to Oberoi´s father who was successful in arranging this equipment for both of us. Nana had a relative in the army, too and could also secure one for himself.

Asia

India

At first we decided to start for the journey on the 20th of October 1954. We had to postpone this date for the 28th October. It was due to the reason that Nana who was working with »All India Radio« could leave by 26th October only. Also between 20th and 27th October there was the Festival Divali and Teeka. (Divali festival is traditionally the New Year Eve for the Hindus and is celebrated with the lights all around the houses and buildings. The festival Teeka is also

From left to right: Ishaq Baluch, Prabhakar Kotwal, Omprakash Virmani

a Hindu tradition where the sisters remind their brothers to look after them and remember them as long as they live by giving a flower garland and sweets).

The night of 27th October was full of tension. To overcome this tension I began to keep together the necessary things like clothes, documents, literature, road maps etc. so that the next day when we had to start nothing important was left back. I had very less or to say practically no sleep. In my mind the scene of departure from my parents went through like a tragic part of a scene where I was trying in mind to search the adequate words for a parting dialogue for my parents.

The morning of **28th October** was a depressive one, in order to overcome such depressive atmosphere I started packing the aforesaid things in my bags and fixed this bags on the bicycle. In the meantime all the friends and neighbours gathered around us and started giving me friendly advises and instructions. It was planned that Ishaq starts from his house and joins me at our place and then we both cycle up, eventually with friends to Nanas place and then all three of us bicycle together towards the General Post Office which was our ultimate starting point. Ishaq came to our place accompanied with his family members. His grandfather was a professional photographer and made lot of photographs of our families as a remembrance. I was standing in the last row for the photograph with my father, mother sister and younger brother, so that others should not notice the tears in my eyes. After departing from all the friends and family members we cycled up to Nanas place. Here also the same scenes took place. Some of our family members and other friends escorted us by bicycles to the starting point.

At the General Post Office members of the World Wide Brotherhood, family members and friend were gathered to give us a grand see off. Some members of the WWB escorted us up to five kilometers from the starting point. Hardly we had travelled ten further kilometres when the first puncture took place. Ishaqs bicycle had to be patched. This patch remained intact for further 60 kilometers. The tube used for Ishaqs bicycle was a special one used with racing cycles, it could not be repaired any further, therefore he had no choice but to take a second hand one from a small repairing shop on the road side. This tube carried him one kilometer only and here we had the third breakdown. Just as we were sitting along the roadside and discussing about the further steps, when a truck passing by stopped next to where we were waiting and asked whether he could give us a lift up to Pavel.

In Pavel we were not successful in securing a tube and the cover which had also been damaged with the bursting of the tube. Therefore Ishaq had no alternative than to try to get a lift by a truck to Bombay. He was lucky to get one, whereas Nana and myself remained there to continue on further by bicycles. Since it was getting dark we cycled round in the town to find out a possibility for overnight. Ultimately we were welcome as free guests in a small hotel in the town. Early next morning Nana and myself continued the journey. We had to cover about 58 Kilometers. After about four hours we reached Bombay.

Bombay

In Bombay we were the guests of the regional Secretary of Youth Hostels Association, Mr. Kamath, who at the same time was the director of the Telang Memorial Student Association. We remained three days in Bombay. During these days we collect-

A group photograph with the home minister Mr. Patil and their Excellencies.

Welcome gathering with the members of WWB in Bombay

The home minister Mr. Patil presenting us all flower garlands

ed the travellers cheques by the agents of »Thos. Cook & Sons«, which we had ordered by their agents in Poona, visited the consulate of Pakistan and applied for the visa to travel through Pakistan by road with bicycles. We were told that this visa shall be handed over to us by their High commissioners office at the border city of Jullunder.

Mr. Pochkhanawala (WWB) holding a welcome speech

The Association of World Wide Brotherhood had organised a grand see-off for three of us and had invited the Home Minister of the Bombay state Mr. Patil and the consular representatives of Saudi-Arabia, Iraq, Great-Britain, West Germany and over fifty members of the Association. The send off celebration was inaugurated in the Congress Centre, where Mr. Patil presided the celebration. According to Indian tradition we were presented with flower garlands. In his address Mr.

Cyclists On World Tour

BOMBAY, Saturday.

THREE graduates of the Poona Engineering College will leave Bombay on November 2 on a world tour on cycles. They will return to India in 1960.

The three cyclists — Baluch, Kotwal and Om Prakash — were today given a reception by the Wide World Club, Bombay.

They will visit Pakistan, Afghanistan, Iran, Iraq, Israel, Turkey, Greece, Yugoslavia, Italy, Switzerland, Finland, Germany, Denmark, Holland, France, Spain, Portugal and England and then cross the Atlantic to pedal through America and Canada.

While in Europe and America, the three young men will serve as apprentices in some leading tele-communication companies.

Shri S. K. Patil, President of the Bombay Pradesh Congress Committee, presiding over the reception stressed the need for encouraging the "spirit of travel among the youth of the country."

Shri Patil said that travel was the best method of creating goodwill and peace among nations. PTI.

THE BHARAT JYOTI
SAT. 30th Oct 1954

રવીવાર, તા૦ ૩૧ મા ઓક્ટોબર, ૧૯૫૪.

સાઇકલ પર દુનિયાના પ્રવાસે નીકળેલા ત્રણ નવયુવાનો

ધી વાઇડ વર્લ્ડ બ્રધરહુડ તરફથી ત્રણેય યુવાનોને અપાયેલી વિદાય

(અમારા પ્રતિનિધિ તરફથી).

મુંબઈ, તા૦ ૩૦ મી ઓકટોબર.

મી૦ બલુચ, મી૦ કોટવાલ અને મી૦ ઓમપ્રકાશ નામના પુનાના ત્રણ યુવાનો સાઈકલ પર દુનીઆની મુસાફરીએ નીકળ્યા છે. આ ત્રણેય યુવાનોએ ઈજનેરીની ડીગ્રી મેળવી છે અને દુનીઆના પ્રવાસ દરમ્યાન, ઈજનેરીના વીષયમાં તાલીમ મેળવવાનો તેમનો ઈરાદો છે. આ સંબંધમાં વીદેશોના કેટલાક મોટા ઈજનેરીના કારખાનાંનો તેમણે સંપર્ક પણ સાધ્યો છે અને તેમને એ કારખાનાં તરફથી પુરતી સગવડ આપવાની ખાતરી પણ મળી છે.

આ ત્રણેય યુવાનો સાથે મી૦ ઈરાની નામના એક ચોથા યુવાન પણ વિશ્વની સફર માટે જોડાનાર હતા પરંતુ છેક છેલ્લી ઘડીએ મી૦ ઈરાનીએ તેમનો વિચાર પડતો મુકયો હતો. મી૦ બલુચ, મી૦ કોટવાલ અને મી૦ ઓમપ્રકાશ તા૦ ૨૮ મી ઓકટોબરે પુનાથી ઉપડીને મુંબઈ આવ્યાં છે અને તા૦ ૨ જી નવેમ્બરે નવી દીલ્હી ભણી ઉપડી જનાર છે.

Patil encouraged us for our adventure, however, reminded us of our responsibility as ambassadors of the our country and wished us all the best for this good-will tour. All the guests present wished us good luck for the long journey. After this send-off celebration we named our journey as »Goodwill Tour« Ishaq in our name thanked Mr. Patil, the consular representatives and last not least the members of the W.W.B.

1st. November was my 24th Birthday. Ishaq gave a birthday party at his uncles place. A knife made specially for me in the work shop of his uncle was my birthday present. The same evening Ishaq declared that he shall not be accompanying us, because he had some personal things to clarify and shall join us at Nasik by train. We were invited by the uncle of Mr. Oberoi who was running a small restaurant in Kasara. Since we had to overcome lot of steep climbs of the road we covered 65 kilometers only by late afternoon. A generous Jeep driver took mercy on us and gave us a lift up to Thana. Further 22 kilometers we reached Kasara in the evening. We remained there for the night and enjoyed the hospitality of Mr. Oberoi.

Next morning after a grand breakfast we were again on the road toward Nasik. The road was plane and there were not many steep climbs. We were at a high point from where we could see a vast green valley around us. With such pleasant impressions we travelled with good speed and reached Nasik in the evening. In Nasik we were expected by the relatives of Ishaq who observed conservative Moslem traditions and moved in the house covered from the guests. A person of the family escorted us through the house, where the female members were warned with verbal sounds to move away in other rooms. Late afternoon Nana and myself went to take a bath in the river Narvada, where lot of pilgrims come all the year along to so called wash their sins in the holy waters.

In the evening Ishaq joined us. We had a sleepless night because the famous bugs were all around. Early next morning we proceeded for Malegaon. The road was straight but we had strong opposite wind and after some time it was pretty hot to cycle on. Mighty tired we reached Malegaon. The first task was to find a place for the night. We asked someone about any church in the city and were directed to the one in the city. On the way to the church we saw a new building little farther on and asked someone about it and were informed that it was the building of the new school »Gandhi Vidya Vidyala«. Instead going to the church we headed towards this building. There was a meeting of delegates from different parts of Maharashtra State to discuss the problems of education in the state. The Agriculture Minister of Maharashtra Mr. Punjab Rao Deshmukh was invited to do the opening ceremony for the new built school. Luckily we were just in time to meet him before he left after the inauguration ceremony of the new school. I could obtain his autograph. He wished us good luck for the journey. This meeting with the delegates was fruitful for us so that we were allowed to remain there with other delegates. Also we were allowed to attend the meeting without taking part for the discussion.

We remained an additional day in Malegaon because Ishaq had some work to settle at Chalisgaon, a town not lying on our route. He came back the next day and so we proceeded for the next station Dhulia. We reached Dhulia in the afternoon, here we tried to contact one of our professors, who was now the principal of Dhulia Technical College. Unfortunately he was out of station, therefore after having our meals in the student canteen we proceeded further for Shirpur, a town about 32 kilometers from Dhulia. Since we felt tired and lazy after the meals in the students canteen, we found a place in one of the vacant house and took rest for about two hours.

We were just on the road when a truck passing by stopped on our request and gave us a lift for 15 kilometers and then refused to take us further being afraid of RTO (Regional Traffic Officer).

We remained in the small town and after some time proceeded further. Though it was late in the evening but since the full moon was out we could follow the road with our bicycle head lights and reached Shirpur, a small town with about 6000 inhabitants. We were told that the town was often flooded during heavy rainfall, specially in the monsoon season. Once the whole town had to be vacated due to floods where the people had to live in tents and returned after the level of water had fallen. The maximum height of the water was marked on a pole in the middle of town. We remained there for the night and proceeded further to Phalghat about 128 kilometers from Shirpur. Phalghat is the city on the border of Bombay and Madhya Pradesh States. A truck driver gave us a lift up to the border. On the way the driver told us that mostly the truck drivers cross the border to Madhya Pradesh at midnight and return loaded for Bombay by midnight the same day so that they return within the same day and thus save taxes. While we were waiting at the border of the state we noted that many truck drivers were waiting for the night so that they could start. They agreed to give us a lift provided we waited till the night. Since we were curious of such adventure we agreed to wait to be carried up to Indore.

Around the border it was a hilly place down below a stream of clear and cold water and a small temple aside. We regarded the place an ideal one for a picnic, we had a bath in the stream and then had our meals at one of the restaurants run specially for the truck drivers. After the meals we had a nap in the temple. We had long talk with the drivers to get an insight into their activities of life. We found out that the drivers are a tough lot who for a long period get along without much food and sleep and are most of the time on the road. The exchange of information between the drivers and ourselves was very fruitful for us. As a result of this conversation more than one truck driver wished to give us the lift. We ultimately agreed with one driver and as a remembrance took the photograph of the border stone on which a bottle with a cross was engraved indicating that in Bombay state prohibition was imposed.

Both Ishaq and Nana got on the truck and made themselves comfortable on top of the load whereas I joined the driver and his co.-driver in the cabin. We sang throughout the night all possible songs to keep us awake. By early in the morning we arrived in Indore. We all slept for sometime after arrival. After waking up we all three thanked the driver.

Nana had a friend in Indore so we went in search of the house of Mr. Menezes. After a long searching we found the house. Mr. and Mrs. Menezes were very hospitable and gave us a grand feeding. They insisted that we should stay at least one more day in Indore. Mr. Narian Karindikar, a classmate of Nana was sent to Indore for the installation of a radio transmitting station. We spent the day with him. He showed us the palace, the temples and the big gardens in the city.

Next morning after a grand breakfast with the family Menezes we proceeded towards Ujjain. This city was out of the way from the main road. We bicycled up to Dewas and then across to Ujjain. The road was full of holes and small ditches. On arriving in Ujjain we were surrounded by lot of spectators, who were very curious to know about us. As usual we tried to answer all the questions put to us. Being earthquake area Ujjain was destroyed by lava. The worth seeing places were the old ruins of the city and lot of temples being a holy city and of course the Kalida palace. Unfortunately due to shortage of time we could not make it to visit all these places and after some rest proceeded further.

The road from Ujjain to Maksi was a horrible experience. After half the way to Maksi the road improved. The moon had just appeared in the sky and so we continued our journey to reach Maksi the same night. Late evening we reached Maksi and were making plans to rest for the night in a travellers bungalow just then a truck stopped next to us and asked us whether we wished to join him to Shajapur. We regarded this as a grand opportunity and this way reached Shajapur. Since it was still dark and furthermore we did not see any chance to secure a possibility for the night we decided to sleep at the custom house. We were informed by the custom officer that every truck going toward Gawalior had to stop there to pay the taxes. We thought if we remained there we have good chances for getting a lift up to Gawalior.

After getting up in the morning we found that we had left the army water bottle in Maksi. Since it was not possible to buy such a bottle Ishaq decided to hitch hike back to Maksi to get the bottle. He was lucky to get the bottle and returned in the afternoon. Consequently we decided to remain in Shajapur till the evening where we had chances to get a lift in the trucks leaving towards Gwalior. While we were waiting a Sikh gentleman invited us to be his guest. In the evening we got a lift by a truck heading towards Gwalior.

About 8 kilometers before Biora a caltex truck had fallen over the bridge in the river below. The truck driver stopped and we got down and on enquiring came to know that the truck driver himself was unhurt because he had fallen into the river but the co.-driver was injured seriously and nobody dared to help him. Since our truck was the next on the scene we were requested to help and take the injured person to the hospital. At first our truck driver hesitated to help with a remark »It serves them right« because both the unhurt driver and the injured co.-driver were drunk. But after we insisted he agreed to help. So we three of us covered the injured person in a blanket and carried him up in the truck and then brought him to the next hospital. Thereafter the truck driver continued the journey towards Gawalior.

The sun was high and it was getting pretty warm on the truck, so we took a piece of canvas and tied it such a way that it looked like a camping tent. By noon we reached Guna. The driver needed a nap for a while, because he had been driving right from 12.00 p.m. We took this opportunity and took a short swim in the river. After everybody was ready we started further. The driver told his life story that as a boy of 12 he had to leave his parents house to work and that he had been lucky to learn driving and had so far no contact with his family. It seemed that he found his life useless. He regarded his truck as his friend, as his wife and so on. He had spent quite a good amount of money for decorating his truck with photographs of Indian actors and actresses and the mythological goddesses and gods.

At night we reached Shivpuri. Here the driver had to collect the goods to be transported to Gawalior. Unfortunately the contractor, a Gujrati fellow, could not deliver the goods at night and therefore we had to stay overnight at Shivpuri. We all except Nana and the co.-driver slept in a theatre which was closed down as a result of a quarrel between the two brothers, who agreed to disagree on many things.

Next morning we helped the contractor to deliver his goods to be loaded on the truck, so that we could all proceed on. It was late afternoon when everything was loaded and we proceeded further. We reached Gwalior late in the evening. We thanked the driver and moved towards Morar, a suburb of Gwalior, where Mr. Agarwal, who had met Ishaq three years back would be our host. We had a very warm welcome by Mr. Agarwal and were his guests for three days. In these three days we visited a most modern biscuit manufacturing factory with magnificent packing design to promote the sales of biscuits.

Our host also showed us round the Agarwal Mills, where he was the Assistant Manager of the Mills. He arranged a grand party for his friends so that we could meet quite a number of people. Also he gave us a recommendation letter so that we could visit J.C. Mills, a Birla concern. A guide escorted us through the mills and showed us the various stages of production, quality control and the work facilities for the workers and the management. The mill was very vast it took us half the day seeing around the mills. The visit left a good impression on us that hardly seven years after the independence of India we could visit one of the most modern manufacturing plant which could in our opinion compete with similar plants in Europe.

The same night Ishaq left for Jhansi to settle some private affairs. Nana and myself spent the time to visit the Gwalior fort. In the fort there were three things worth seeing from the ancient time: the Sas Bhahi Temple, Man Singh Temple and the Sheesh Mahal (Palace with glass pieces embedded on the walls). A lot of visitors were there to see these ancient relics.

At the Gwalior gate end there was a museum of all the old monuments and portraits from the early Gupta time. In the bazaar we could locate the tomb of Tansen, a famous singer during the period of Akbar dynasty. The tomb had no particular surrounding, no flowers or any such decoration.

The next morning Ishaq returned from Jhansi and after thanking our host we proceeded towards Agra. We had a strong opposite wind and therefore could not travel faster as planned by us. By evening we had covered about 80 kilometers and had still about 40 kilometers to go. We switched our cycle dynamos on and continued the journey. We reached Agra at about 9.00 p.m. We could note that some sweet-meat shops were open. Each of us drank a glass of hot milk and ate some sweets. Now we started to search for a place to sleep. We saw a bungalow but were hesitant to ask the owner for the shelter. We then went to the District Board Office. We seeing it to be a clean place decided to remain there for the night, but as we entered the area, the night guard asked us to leave the place. In the meantime some more people joined the night guard. Looking at our outfit they very soon recognized us as the cycle tourists who had helped the co.-driver who had met with an accident at Biora. However, they could not help us. We ultimately went to the Hindu-Hospice, where we had the company of two more persons without shelter and a dog.

In the morning we went in search of a friend of Nana with a hope to be accommodated for the night. After a long searching we found the house but he too having a big family could not accommodate us. I remembered that I had a very far distant relative of mine living in Agra, who had a leather goods-shop. After some searching we found the place. After I met the said person and explained to him our situation, he at once invited us to be his guests.

We stayed with them for two days. During the day of our arrival we rested in the house because we had not slept well the night before. In the afternoon we decided to visit Taj Mahal. A monument built by the Mogul king Shahajahan for his wife Noorjahan, which was built by many experts from different countries of orient in twenty two years. The period required to build this monument is indicated by 22 turrets on top of the entrance gate. This monument is built with white marble stone and looks very enchanting and romantic specially in the moon light.

During our visit to Taj Mahal we met two American girls touring in India. During our conversation we realised that they had very less knowledge about America. They were visiting India because they had chosen »India« as subject for their higher studies. After saying good bye we returned to the house.

Next morning after a good breakfast we said good bye to our host and proceeded for Mathura. We reached there in the afternoon and were just searching for a restaurant to take our meals when a gentleman seeing our outfit came forward and greeted us. He became inquisitive about our mission and to inform himself invited us for lunch. He promised to guide us round the city of Mathura. A place with 3000 temples. With our well versed guide we visited few of the well known temples and then said good bye to the unknown gentleman and proceeded further towards Vrindraban a town with 1000 Shrines.

Hardly we were one kilometer from Mathura when Pandas (Brahmans who feel responsible to take all the visitors round to most of the temples) accompanied us promising to show us all the important temples and shrines, we had heard before that when these Pandas do not get appreciable money for their services they start quarrelling with you. To avoid such situation we visited two temples only and then decided to proceed on to Aligarh. We took a fairy to the other side of river Jammuna and continued our journey. It was not the main road but a small rough road leading to the main road. After about 5 kilometers we reached the main road.

At Raya we met a teacher of the school, who invited us to stay for the night at Raya. Since we had to reach Aligarh the same night we thanked him for the invitation and proceeded further. It was getting darker, we switched on our bicycle-dynamos and reached a railway crossing where we drank some water. The officer in charge warned us that the way to Aligarh was not safe to travel at night. We ignored the warning and continued on. We made a stop in a small place called Mersan.We were hungry and took some food in the road side restaurant. Here again we were warned. Not ignoring such a warning we decided to stay for the night in the temple rest house, where we were accommodated with all the facilities.

Early next morning we proceeded for Aligarh. On the way a milkman met us and during our conversation came to know that we had rested the night at Mersan. He felt sorry that we did not come to the next village where he would have taken care of us. He told us that since his elder brother died in the 2nd world war he now being the younger brother was looking after his and also his brothers family. He filled our water bottle with milk. We stopped in a roadside snack shop. People waiting there just got round us and asked about our mission. We gave them the usual explanations. With great difficulty we left the place and continued our journey and reached Aligarh by afternoon.

After reaching Aligarh we went straight to the university and asked about the residence address of Mr. Nurullah, the vice chancellor of the University. Ishaq and myself knew Mr. Nurulla and his son and daughter (a twin) from back in Poona, where both the son and the daughter were students in the same college. At the residence we had a very courteous welcome. After we had some tea, Mr. Nurulla gave us a short historical review of the university.

The Aligarh university was founded in 1809 by Sir Sayed Ahmed an educationalist. The university was at first restricted for Muslim students of India only, but now 25% of the students are foreign students specially from Indonesia. On the day of our arrival there was the function of the student union federation. We were allowed to attend the function. The secretary of the federation invited us for tea. At the function we were introduced to a chemist from USA. A black student, who was in India for a long time working his way out. He was deadly against the USA universities which had not admitted him as a student because of his colour. Next day we were shown around the university. In the evening we accompanied our host to attend the diamond Jubilee of Sir Shaik Abdulla, who had devoted his whole life for the education of women successfully. With all these impressions we parted from our host the next day and started for Delhi. As his contribution Mr. Nurulla gave us some money for the way.

The road was favourable. We reached Bulandshahr. A truckdriver gave us a lift up to Hapur from there we cycled up to Delhi. We reached Delhi late in the evening and were relieved to have covered the first stage of our journey. Our plan was to stay for few days in Delhi.

Delhi

Ishaq and Nana went to stay with Dr. Nawathe at Karol Bagh and I went to stay with my uncle. Next day we decided to visit the first youth hostel built by students only. It was not yet completed, but it looked very promising so that in future a lot of young people could get shelter there and as such meet the youth from other nations. The following day we went to the Pakistan Embassy, to find out the possibilities for a visa to travel by road in Pakistan. They were ready to give us an ordinary visa to travel by all other means than by road and by bicycles. However, they promised to try for the said visa after negotiating with their Foreign Office in Karachi. We requested them to send the ultimate decision to their commissioners office in Jullundur.

I took the opportunity to visit my elder brother residing in Dehra Dun and to say good bye to him and his family. I travelled by train. I stayed six days with my brothers family. During this time we also made a trip to Mussoorie hill station about 2720 meters high. Here the far away range of Himalaya mountains full of snow presented a pleasant scenery. The trucks were not allowed at this area. Mostly the loads were carried by Gadwalis (Sherpas, who carry all kinds of load from 1000 up to 3000 meters height). Lots of Europeans stayed at Mussoorie which has lot of gardens, parks etc.

Ishaq and Nana were waiting anxiously for my return. The newspapers were full of reports about us. From Aligargh we had written to the offices of the Prime Minister of India, Mr. Jawahar lal Nehru and the President of India Mr. Rajendra Prasad for a short presentation so as to have a moral support from the highest representative of the country, but we did not get any reply. So we decided to resume our journey towards India-Pakistan-border. We had taken contacts with the representatives of the embassy of Iran, Iraq, Syria, Jordan and so on and explained to them about our good will tour to their country, thereby of course hoping that we may get the necessary visas free of charge for these countries. All the same we had tough time getting a recommendation letters from the said representatives. On 3rd. December 1954 we got a recommendation letter from the representatives of Iran, Iraq, Syria for a visa to be obtained at Karachi.

We then decided to proceed towards Ambala the same night. It was planned that I should meet Ishaq and Nana at Dr. Nawathe´s place and then we should travel further together. After saying good bye to my uncle, aunt and the cousins I cycled up to Dr. Nawathe's house in Karol Bagh. From there we started towards the outskirts of Delhi and stopped at the custom post where we were expecting to get a lift by a truck going up to Karnal. It was rather late at night when we reached Karnal. We thanked the driver and went in search of a place to sleep for the night. We could not find a better place than near a petrol filling station, opened our sleeping bags and went to sleep. Early in the morning we got out of our sleeping bags and cycled further towards Ambala. A milkman carrying seven big cans of milk on a bicycle accompanied us and on the way related to us about his daily life. He left us after few kilometers. We reached Ambala in the afternoon.

We were near the railway station, when a group of people out of curiosity gathered round us. A Sikh gentleman, who had read about us in the newspapers came forward and volunteered to guide us to the news papers office. We reached the P. T. I.(Press Trust of India) and the offices of the Tribune. The chief journalist of Tribune inquired about the object of our tour and then sort of cross examined us. On finding the limit of our finances doubted whether we would really manage with the amount we were carrying each. Thereafter he invited us for a good lunch. The object of his invitation was to discuss with us the details of our journey. After hearing our story he gave us quite some instructions and above that Rupees 20,- as his contribution for the journey. He introduced us to the director of Sanatan Dharam College and arranged that we were accommodated in the college hostel. The same day there was a function to be inaugurated at the hostels. A yogi was going to demonstrate that one has his muscles and the breathing system under control by practising Yoga. By practising meditation and training programme one can keep oneself healthy and above that have peace of mind.

The yogi appeared on the scene. A muscular man with upper naked body and having big beard then gave a demonstration for the press and the people. First of all lot of broken glass pieces were put on a blanket the yogi lied on it and asked to put a big size of wooden board on him and then a tractor was driven on it. With his stomach muscles he shook the tractor up and down. After removal of the tractor and the board the yogi stood up showing his back round where no sign of bleeding was noticed.

We were impressed from this demonstration but had no intention to follow the Yogi. During our stay in the hostel we made a lot of friends. We thanked the director of the College and started further towards Ludhiana. Originally our plan was to go directly to Ludhiana. However, when we reached Rajpura a Sikh gentleman invited us to take some tea with him. We accepted his invitation. While we were taking the tea a police constable joined us and as such out of curiosity many more people around us. The Sikh gentleman convinced us to travel further via Patiala, Maler Kotla, because Patiala is really worth seeing place. We then decided to go via Patiala.

The wind was terrific rather not in favour of us. A Sikh truck driver took pity on us and gave us a lift up to Patiala. On the way the driver told us about his life and that he has travelled practically most of the middle east countries. On reaching Patiala the brother of the truck driver escorted us to the Palace of the Maharaja of Patiala.

We were introduced to the Secretary of the Maharaja. He asked us to wait. After one hour or so the Military attaché of the Maharaja came out and apologised that the Maharaja was rather busy that day and probably see us the next day. We then proceeded towards the College to try to get the accommodation for the night. On the main gate of the College we asked a fellow student about the College hostel. He was very helpful and straight away guided us to the hostel warden, who turned out to be the coach of the Indian National Hockey team. He accommodated us in the reading room. The room was closed for the period of our stay for other students. We visited the city in the company of students.

In the evening we were introduced to the principal of the college, who allowed us to have the meals in the hostel mess as long as we stayed in Patiala. We had the opportunity to see a hockey match between Punjab police and the team of Mohinder College. We had become the centre of attraction. Anywhere and everywhere we stopped there was a group of students around us asking about our plans. Ishaq and Nana purchased the Punjabi shoes for the national dress which we all three were carrying along with us. Our wish to meet the Maharaja of Patiala could not be fulfilled, therefore we decided to proceed further to Nabha. A student who had accompanied us all the time in Patiala wished to join us up to Nabha, where his parents lived. We did not stop at Nabha, thanked our companion and proceeded further to Maler Kotla.

Maler Kotla is a muslim town. Though all the town states have been merged into big state areas, yet Maler Kotla still exists in its original form. The streets are very narrow difficult for the trucks to pass through the narrow city lanes. We were just crossing the road in the main bazaar when two gentleman, eventually professors in the college recently opened, invited us to visit their college. They introduced us to the principal of the new college. After the visit we had a grand meal together. Thereafter we decided to proceed further and left for Ludhiana and reached there late in the evening.

The locating of the college was cumbersome, however we were successful in finding the hostel of the college. We were guided by one of the students to the hostel warden, who we believe had already read about our venture and with pleasure accommodated us in the Gymkhana hostel. Next morning we were introduced to the secretary of the students union. He was very keen to discuss with us the Kashmir problem and other political aspects which he thought to be of importance. We had decided to take a neutral position and therefore did not take part in the discussion.

The following day after thanking the warden of the hostel and other friends we proceeded towards Jullundur. We were just cycling up leisurely when a little further on we saw a big mast. We became inquisitive and entered the area. To our surprise it was the transmitter station of Jullundur Radio Station. The engineer in charge after knowing our qualification gladly agreed to show us around. We took this opportunity to exchange our general and technical views. We thanked our host and proceeded further towards Jullundur. Late in the evening we reached Jullundur.

In Jullundur we had the plans to stay with my eldest sisters family. In the dark it was difficult to locate the residence. With the help of the people on the street we ultimately reached my sisters house. We were heartily welcomed. It was a pleasure for me to meet my sister after a very long time. We all three stayed with them for six days. During this period we visited the magnificent palace at Kapurthala, though a visit to the palace was not allowed, but we being world tourists got special permission to visit the palace. All the rooms in the palace were furnished harmoniously. Also we visited the shrine of Dera Baba and the mosque.

Kashmir

Since a decision by the Pakistan consular authorities for a visa to travel by road through Pakistan i.e. from Lahore, Multan and Quetta to Iran was not yet taken, we planned to visit Kashmir, a state under the foot

A photograph with the truck driver

Warming up with pickaxe after a night in the tent

of Himalayas with a wide beautiful valley and the Dal Lake with its bathing boats. The population constitutes Kashmiris both Hindus and Muslims with Indogerman language origin. Kashmir has a very moving history. Kashmir was ruled by Muslim rulers followed by Sikh rulers and then by the British and ultimately by the Maharaja of Kashmir and now it was parted between India and Pakistan.

We left the bicycles at my sisters place and decided to hitch hike to Srinagar. We moved towards the outskirts of Jullundur to get a lift to Pathankot. We waited there for a long time without getting a lift. Many trucks passed by but no one stopped. After about two hours a truck stopped and gave us a lift up to the next town. He left us near a sugarcane field. Each of us took a sugarcane and started eating it.

We did not know how far we were from Pathankot, we were just discussing about the next steps, when a train stopped at the station not far away from us. We suddenly decided to take the train and were successful to get into it. Since we could not buy the tickets we were watching for the controller all the time and on every station where the train stopped. Ishaq did not worry about it and went to sleep as soon we had entered the compartment of the train. We had no idea how long the train had been moving. All of a sudden we heard the squeezing noise of the brakes and with a jerk the train stopped. We had reached Pathankot.

When we got out of the station, the city was about a kilometer from the station. We walked up to the city. Here we went in search of a place to sleep. We located a house but since the nightwatchman, who was around, he did not allow us to sleep in the veranda of the house. Ishaq and Nana decided to sleep in a house which was under construction and had no roof. I did not find the place comfortable and went little further on and saw two benches in a veranda of an office and so here I went to sleep on the bench.

At 2.00 a.m. the manager peeped out of the window and saw me sleeping there and woke me up and asked questions who I was etc. After he saw my dress and the way I talked to him he became conciliatory to receive all three of us. He asked us to join him for the breakfast. He told us that in the month of December very few trucks travel towards Srinagar because of cold and bad weather. He then proposed that we should better obtain a permit from the police authorities and then contact a trade agent, whose truck go to Jammu and Srinagar. This way it will be easy to get a lift.

Without any difficulty we got the permit from the police authorities. Thereafter we contacted the said trade agent and introduced ourselves and showed him the permit to travel to Srinagar. On that day there was no truck due to Jammu, so he asked us to wait there and promised to arrange the journey by the truck for us. We stayed there for the night. The next day he arranged such that we could travel with the truck leaving for Jammu. We were five persons on the truck. The driver was pleased to have our company. We came to the border of the state Jammu and Kashmir and showed our permits and continued on.

We had hardly travelled 25 kilometers when the radiator of the truck started leaking. The driver first tried to block the leakage by putting some turmeric powder but it did not work out. There was no other way than to go back to Pathankot and get the radiator repaired. We helped the driver to remove the radiator. He got a lift by another truck back to Pathankot. His co.-driver bought the necessary ingredients and prepared the food. He shared the food with us. We spent the night in a small tent.

Next morning we were pretty stiff due to cold in the tent. Ishaq borrowed the pickaxe from the road worker and started removing the asphalt pavement on the road under repair to get warmed up. Nana and myself tried in turn and then gave up. Thereafter we all sat down to bask in the sun, which had come out. The time passed away soon. In the afternoon again we had the food with the co.-driver. Late in the afternoon the driver returned with the radiator. We helped him to mount it, thereafter the truck started toward Jammu. At 7.00 p.m. we reached Jammu.

It was planned that we shall be the guests of the brother-in law of Nana, who was captain in the Army. It took us about two hours to find the residence of Nana's brother-in-law. We remained there three days.

Now we had to try to get a lift to Srinagar. At first it seemed very difficult to achieve our goal, but then by chance I met a friend of mine, who was my classmate at the Engineering College in Poona. He promised to help us. Just as we were discussing about the possibility when the Army transport officer gave the brother-in law of Nana the information that we could travel by the Army convoy due to leave for Srinagar the same evening.

In the evening it started raining, it was obvious that it would be snowing at the Bahanal Pass at a height of 3250 Meters to Srinagar. We were glad to get such a grand offer and travel with the convoy. Each of us got a place in a different truck next to the driver.The first stop of the convoy was at Udhampur. After arrival all the participants of the convoy got the facility to sleep in a big hall. The drivers knew that the driving upward to Banihal Pass was very tricky and involved a good amount of driving skill because the roads were icy due to the rainfall the day before. The convoy moved on at a speed of 20 to 30 kilometers per hour. One side of the road was the mountain side and the other side without any crash barrier, a tense situation. The drivers were skilled and quite calm and moved on. Late at night we reached Srinagar. What a relief of tension.

We went in search of the hostel of the S. P. College. At last after a long search and guidance of a student we found the hostel. The students accommodated us for the night. It being very cold the students were wearing a long and wide gown under which a clay oven with charcoal fire was carried to warm up the hands. Looked a bit dangerous but the people there were used to it. Nana's brother-in law had given us the address of another captain of the army in Srinagar, whom we should contact after arrival. But since we had reached Srinagar late at night, we decided to contact the captain the next day. For security reasons the army had its own area. Therefore we had no difficulty finding the area and were lucky to meet the said person. He was a jolly fellow and looked after us very nicely.

The following day was left to our disposal. So we visited the Shalimar Gardens, which was set up during the reign of Akbar, the Dal Lake. Though it was cold yet the whole city lying in a valley presented a grand landscape. No wonder they say »It looks like paradise and one should have seen it before one dies.« We went round the market as such the bazaar was full of handicraft work like carpets, brassiere work, silk garments and shawls. We bought few items, so far as our finances allowed it, to be sent to the family at Poona.

In the evening we were awaited by the captain. In the officers mess we were offered a glass of brandy to warm up against cold. Though we were not used to hot drinks, however each of us had an internal desire to experience the kick. After the meal we thanked our host and returned to the hostel.

Our journey back to Jammu was arranged in the same convoy returning to Jammu by our host. Early next morning before the sunrise we were on the road to Jammu. Since the weather was not good, the convoy moved slowly towards Banihal Pass. The night was again passed in a big hall in Udhampur. The next day at 9.00 a.m. we reached Jammu.

The brother-in law of Nana had arranged our transport to Pathankot so we reached the town without any incidents. As usual we could not get the lift further to Jullundur. We stayed for the night in Pathankot. Next morning we decided to travel by train to save time and reached Jullundur comfortably.

During our absence in Jullundur my sister had received the passports from the Pakistan high commissioner in Jullundur, but with an ordinary visa, valid for three months for Lahore, Sukkur and Karachi. Ishaq and Nana decided to start the same day further to Amritsar and then to the border. We packed our bags and fixed them on the bicycles. Then we said good bye to the relatives and friends and started towards Amritsar. On the way we met Rudolph, a German tourist on bicycle. He mentioned that his journey so far has been full of adventure. He told us that in Turkey he had to spend the night in a tent in a field. It rained very heavily for the whole night. In the morning when he got out of his tent he found himself on a meadow. All around his tent was deep water.

The same night we stopped about 29 kilometers from Amritsar and slept in a mill. Next day after reaching Amritsar we visited the golden temple and the »Jallianwalla Bagh« where in 1919 people had demonstrated against the British Government. The British troops had fired into the public killing over 1500 persons, men, women and children. The bullets marks were still visible all around. After the visit to this remarkable historical place we went forward towards the town in search for a place for the overnight. Where ever we went the people gathered around us asking about our journey and the motive of the tour. We got accommodation in the College hostel.

Pakistan

The next day we started towards the border town Attari of India On 30th December 1954 at 11.00 a.m. we crossed over to the border town Wagah in Pakistan. The border police authorities checked very thoroughly our documents and the bags we were carrying. After all these formalities we were allowed to proceeded further to Lahore. Late afternoon we reached Lahore.

Lahore

Originally we had the plan to stay at the Y.M.C.A but a gentleman, Mr. Saleem, met us near Schalimar and invited us to stay in the hostel of the College of Engineering and guided us to the hostel. Since the principal of the College was out, the hostel warden, Mr. Wahid Ali greeted us. It being cold we all sat down on the jute woven cots in the sun. Mr.Wahid arranged for our stay. He asked two students to accompany us to the hostel where we occupied the rooms. In the hostel we met another student who was residing in the hostel and studying in the college for the last 12 years and had not yet completed the studies. He disclosed to us that he had a rich father, who after his death had left lot of money for him. To save money he is staying in the hostel rather than in the city, where the room is expensive.

During our stay he accompanied us to alle the places we intended to visit. Also a tourist society read about our venture. They arranged a sightseeing tour of Lahore for us. We visited »Shahi Masjid« the largest Mosque in Lahore, the fort. The temple built by Maharaja Ranjit Singh was allowed for Sikhs only, who came as visitors from India. We were tourists and had the hope that we shall get the permission but no exception was made for us. In the fort we saw the architecture of Mogul period the »Shiesh Mahal« a Mahal where in the roof and the walls round glass pieces were embedded. An attendant lighted the candles and showed how the whole roof of the room illuminated and looked like shining stars in the sky. Khane Aam (House of commons), Khane khas (House of Lords).

After the breakfast Ishaq and Nana left. I remained in the hostel and was listening to the radio commentary of the cricket match between West Indies and Pakistan. To my surprise the cousin of Ishaq appeared in the threshold of the door. He came all the way from Vazirabad to meet him. Ishaqs cousin informed him that a relative of his father was holding a high position in the Home ministers office. Next day Ishaq contacted the said relative and was surprised to know that his relative had studied in England and was married to an English woman and had three sons. With the help of the said relative of Ishaq the ordinary visa was extended to travel by road to Karachi with the condition that we report on arrival and departure at each place we stopped on our route to the local police authorities.

During our stay in Lahore we had the opportunity to meet the high commissioner of India. He was glad to meet us and declared to help us whatsoever necessary. When we saw the flag of India on the car of the commissioner we got the idea to carry also flags on our bicycles, which could be a help for our good will tour. We requested the high commissioner whether he could help us to this effect. The High Commissioner promised to provide us with the flag of India and also of Pakistan. He did provide us with the flags which we fixed on our bicycles.

After two days we started further towards Montgomery (Sahiwal), our next destination. A group of ten cyclists escorted us about 10 kilometers from the center of the city and after wishing us good journey left. We had cycled 20 kilometers when we felt hungry and took a breakfast in a small shop along the roadside and then started further. We reached Pathoki in the evening. Some people, who had already read about us in the paper came to receive us and insisted to take tea with them and promised to help us in getting a lift by a truck if we remained there for few hours. During this period lot of questions about ourselves and as usual about our motives had to be answered. After about two hours the truck came, we put the cycles and the bags on the truck and after saying good bye were again on the road. We reached Montgomery (Sahiwal) late in the evening.

The driver invited us for the evening meals. In order not to offend him we accepted the invitation. As usual after the meal we went in search for a hostel of a school or College, whatever provision was available in the city. Montgomery is a big city and had a grand College. We met some students and obviously asked them about the address of the warden of the hostel. The students accompanied us to the residence of the warden, who was doing his prayers, so we waited. After he came to know about us he opened a room adjoining the rooms of the students. They all came out and obviously put questions about us and the objectives. We tried our best to give the appropriate answers. Since we were tired we decided to retire and go to sleep.

Next morning we were escorted to the house of the director of the College. He invited us for a breakfast, where we had the opportunity to drink the buffalo milk. During the breakfast he mentioned that he was a member of youth hostels and was very keen for mountaineering in Kashmir etc. Since we had a plan to visit the ancient ruins of the city of Harappa we asked for leave. Before saying good bye we took a photograph with the host. In the meantime the students and the teachers had gathered together to say good bye to us.

To reach the said ruins we had to leave the main road. Just when we left the main road the landscape changed and looked like a desert all around. The road was very narrow. After 20 kilometers we reached the ruins. The excavation of the city had started in 1937 to find out the standard of civilisations that existed there. To our surprise a museum was being set up with all the articles mostly clay pottery which have been recovered intact and also pieces of clay pottery which had to be put together, all neatly kept in row to be adjusted in the museum.

The man in charge of the museum showed us round. He specially showed us the canalisation where the drinking water and the drainage system existed. That means that at the predicted time the separation of drinking and waste water system already existed. The wheel was also known, so that people could carry the load, such as grains from the field to the storage place by bullock carts. It was significant in the ruins that two different civilisations co-existed at the same place where the walls were built by burnt clay bricks. They say that the whole area around was full of woods. All the woods were used for burning the clay bricks, and therefore the whole area was a desert now.

At present the requirement for the woods for burning the clay bricks was covered from north of Pakistan where the tree blocks were recovered out of river Indus. Also there were signs of silos for the storage of grains etc. Also cotton was grown. The man in charge of the museum asked us to visit the ruins of Moenja Daro near the city of Larkana en route to Karachi. We thanked him for the detailed information and proceeded further towards the main road and late afternoon reached Chichawatni.

We went to the main bazaar in search for a restaurant. After the meals we proceeded further. We had cycled up 16 kilometers when the rain started. We saw a big building ahead. It turned out to be a railway station. The station master was kind to let us in the building till the rain stopped. We thanked him and then started further to Khanewal. The roads were very narrow, whenever a truck would pass either from the front side or from behind we had to get down the bicycles. A truck driver took pity on us and asked us if we wanted a lift up to Khanewal. Estimating the situation we gladly accepted the lift. We took seats at the back of the truck. Just after few kilometers a strong wind lifted the hat of Ishaq and it just flew away. We had to stop the truck to pick up the hat. Fortunately it was not damaged by the following traffic. The travelling made us hungry and therefore after reaching Khanewal we took some food in a small restaurant along the roadside. A police constable also taking food there became anxious and came over and put us lot of questions. When he noted that our documents were all right he left us alone. A person who was the witness of the situation came forward and as a compensation for this check by the police paid our bills.

Though it was late in the evening we decided to continue and late in the evening reached Multan. We stopped to drink hot milk at one of the shop. A well dressed man, who seemed to be a teacher was waiting at the shop and was keen to meet us and after having received satisfactory answers to his questions invited us for a feed and thereafter wished to be our guide for a visit of the old Fort of Multan. He knew the shopkeeper and asked him to look after our bicycles etc. We kept our bicycles and the bags at the shop and accompanied the man to visit the Fort of Multan which was very famous during the British rule. In this Fort a mosque and a temple existed together. Since it was a full moon night it all looked very romantic. After the visit the gentleman invited us to be his guest for the night.

Next morning during the breakfast we came to know that a new road had been built between Lahore and Karachi, which was not indicated in the road map that we were carrying along. We were told that the road over Muzaffargarh was the proper one. We took this road. When we reached Muzaffargarh, I noticed that Dera Ghazi Khan was only 50 kilometers over the river Sindh.

Since my ancestors came from Dera Ghazi Khan, at this moment I remembered how we used to cross the river Sindh by a boat driven by steam shovel to spend summer vacations with our parents at the grandfathers house before the partition of India in 1947. An overwhelming feeling came to my mind and I proposed my companions with an appeal to visit the city and may be I could visit the house of the grandfather which he had built for his family. In addition to that the house had a particular significance because the grandfather had to build the house partly himself at the present place after the river Sindh had changed its route. After crossing the river over a temporary wooden bridge supported by boats. We continued the journey by road. Late in the afternoon we reached Dera Ghazi Khan.

As soon as we reached the city many people gathered around us. A rumour went round that a person living in the city before the partition of India is in the town. They greeted me very enthusiastically. After we had our meals at one of the restaurants I requested Ishaq and Nana to accompany me to the area where according to my remembrance the house of our ancestors was or should be.

We were on our way for the search of the house, when a policeman stopped us and asked us for our passports. Since he couldn't read English he asked us to follow him to the police station. At the police station the sergeant responsible was not at the station. After he came he expressed his inability to read English and thus asked us to wait for the security officer who was responsible for such cases. After the security officer arrived, he at once recognised us and said that he had been reading about us in the newspapers and asked us whether he could help us. He told us that we should not worry about any reporting etc.

Not expecting any further difficulties we left the police station and cycled up to the bazaar. There we met a person who knew the vicinity of the ancestors house and accompanied us. At last we found the house. When I knocked on the door a person appeared in the door. After explaining to him who I was, I asked for permission to enter the house. At first he hesitated but then another person appeared in the threshold and he let me in.

The house was built by my grandfather for his four sons. All these four parts were occupied by four different families. We took a photograph in front of the house, a person watching us came forward and introduced himself. He told us that he was doing a research work about the names of the people who lived there before the partition and the history of the town.

Just in this moment a person from the Intelligence department appeared on the scene. When we told him that we had the permission of the security officer, he left us alone and wished us all the best for further journey. We did not want to loose more time, so we continued the journey. We met two persons, who invited us to stay with them. We thanked them for the invitation but decided to continue on in order not to have further significant trouble with the police.

The moon was out, a truck stopped and gave us a lift up to Jampur. It was dark everywhere and no person on the road or around to be seen. We were just standing there and wondering as what should be done when we heard in the distance somebody singing. We reached a house and saw the light inside and knocked on the door. A person opened the door when he saw us he asked us to come in the house. After he came to know about our venture he gave us a big feed and arranged for our beds. We were very tired and went to sleep soon.

Next morning during the breakfast we came to know that our host was a very rich farmer owing vast land. We thanked our host and were again on the road. The road was in very good condition. In the afternoon we reached Mithankot. Here we had our meal at one of the road restaurants and drank as usual in this area lot of hot milk. Since our stomachs very pretty full we formally wished if some passing by truck would give us a lift. As they say that sometimes the dreams come true when you have drunk cow milk. A truck was waiting few hundred meters away from us we hurried up to it and asked the driver for a lift, when I talked to driver and told him my name he started talking to me in my mother language and gladly agreed to give us lift up to Chacharan.

We now entered Bahawalpur state and cycled on to Khanpur and reached there late in the evening. Since there was no signboard at the entrance of the city we went straight to the railway station and inquired there the location of a school in the city. When we reached the school the director was not in but we got the accommodation in the hostel of the school. As usual the students were very curious to know more about ourselves and our journey. We took this opportunity to give a short review of our aim, the way we had covered the way and the experiences we had made so far. After we had said good bye to the director and the fellow students we started further towards our next destination.

We reached the next city Kot Samaba. We were just crossing the city when a man stopped us and introduced himself to be a teacher of the local school and invited us to come to the school. After arrival in the school we were given a warm welcome, also the director and the students came to meet us. Ishaq was fascinated from sugar canes laying there and asked for few pieces of same. They gave him in all 20 pieces. We carried these on the carrier of the cycles. We were asked to answer questions in the school class. We tried our best to answer the questions satisfactorily. After having a meal we were on the road again. In the afternoon we reached Rahimyar Khan. Here a truck gave us a lift up to the highway to Karachi. On the way we reached a place where a tent was fixed on the roadside. There we asked the people sitting in the tent whether Mirpur was on this highway. They told us that for Mirpur we had to leave the highway. One of the gentleman accompanied us up to Umarkot. He also arranged for our food in a small roadside restaurant, but ultimately asked us to pay the bill. Since it was late in the evening and it was getting dark, we slept next to the shop. Next morning the shopkeeper wanted us to pay for the overnight. We had not much cash money in the pocket. We tried to explain the shopkeeper about our aim of the journey, but it was difficult to convince him. Ultimately he accepted not to ask for the money. We now proceeded further for Ghotki, from where onwards it was planned to meet the relatives of Ishaq in a small village by the name Dad Lighari. We reached the place and met the relatives of Ishaq. Since for a very long time we did not have a chance to take a bath we were guided to a Well lying outside the premises of the house where the water was drawn by the Oxes. After the lunch we were escorted to the next village, where Ishaqs uncle resided with his family. We remained with the family for four days.

During this time we had the chance to do the horse riding, hunting etc. I could not join them for hunting because I had fever. Ishaqs buttock was wounded by riding the horse without the saddle. After an enjoying grand hospitality and rest of four days we parted from our hosts and came back to the main road to Mirpur.

In the evening we reached Mirpur. Here we reported to the police authorities because we had during our journey left the main road. After reporting we proceeded towards Sukkur. By late in the evening we reached a small town called Pano Aqil. During our meals we met a person who was helpful in providing the address of the hostel of the school in the town, later on it turned out that the said person was an officer of the Intelligence Department. He arranged for our stay in the hostel. In the evening the idea struck to us to travel further by train to Sukkur, we changed our mind when we came to know the fare, however we decided to go on by bicycles. In the morning we continued on to Sukkur and reached there in the afternoon. We went round the city. During this round we saw a hotel and went inside to take some food. From outside it appeared to be a clean hotel but when we went inside we saw chicken bones, fish bones and similar dirty rests lying around. We took our food quickly and got rapidly out of the hotel. When I got out I noticed that the belt of my bag was broken. Luckily the shoe repair shop was opposite to the hotel and I got it repaired.

Camel cart in Karachi

While we were going round the city we noticed that some British technicians were working there. After enquiring we were told that they had found natural gas resources and as such pipe lines were installed to supply the gas to Karachi. We had no intention to remain there any further and moved towards the main road with the hope to get a lift up to Karachi. We saw a truck waiting on the main road and asked him for a lift, the driver suggested that we should ask the manager of the company who run these trucks. We went to the office of the company and on enquiring got a positive answer.

Nana left with his bicycle and bags with the first truck going to Hydrabad. Ishaq left with the next truck. I was still waiting at the office of the company and was introduced to the member of the corporation.

Bharati Cyclists Pass Through Pakistan

about three months now, ·ft our home and started on ▸ During the last three :·covered a couple of thou- on our bicycles and another r so on trucks. With all those ıd us we have finished with 'ak sub-continent.

tarted becoming mem- ıe different organisations ıld likely be helpful to us route. These were, "Y.M. ɘ Wide World Brotherhood" Youth Hostels Associations The first one is well-known. ı is a brother-hood sponsored ıgazine "The Wide World" ·ople interested in travel and are on the list of 'Brothers'. 'Brothers' in practically all he world, and they help us · t··r.

ne, the Youth Hostels affiliated to the Inter- · Federation, and they ing youth by offering ı accommodation. The ıot very strong in In- ..... but on the Continent ing fine. We wish a hostel is ·in Pakistan and the Indian ·ill be most willing to offer a nd.

ıok our ordinary visa for ıkkur and Karachi and hore in the afternoon of the ber 195 4, with mixed feel- as my first day out of In- ·e wo... ondering what sort were ces were in store for us in

after spending about a Pakistan we are happy to ·e had very pleasant time in ry. We enjoyed the true spitality which this country ılly and rightly boasts of. We people belonging to all clas- ·ty. In Lahore we were with ·ering students of the Gov- ngineering College and that ıere very much reminded us ge days. We celebrated the Lahore and after obtain- ı permission to paddle our gh Pakistan.

r way, we crossed the river ·ı to Dera Gazi Khan from ıaddled along the other bank ill we reached Mia Channu once again crossed the river ıahawalpur State

ıd we spent four days with ıis in a small village called ıbli' on the outskirts of the ıple of that remote village ·ı and hardy. But their appearance was deceptive for inside their rough exterior they seemed to nest a very kind heart. Of course one has to live their way of life to penetrate their exterior.

Next thing to be seen along our route was the Sukkur Barrage, so very famous throughout the country. The volumes of water flowing through the canals on the two banks of the river gave us great satisfaction for that water was on its way to convert vast stretches of desert into a garden.

Another interesting thing we noticed at Sukkur was the Sui Gas Transmission line. The Sui Gas is a great find for this country. As they say, it can keep going all the stationary boilers in Pakistan for a hundred years. Any amount of energy is yours, just for the tapping. But one thing made us rather uneasy and that was the lack of Pakistanis working on the project. One can very well understand the reason for that. But all the same it does prick.

In Karachi we expected to have rest. But we would hardly do anything of the sort because, we met a number of enthusiasts here and we had to give them some of our time. Moreover, we had to fix up our visas for the countries of the Middle East and we are glad that all those countries issued 'Gratis' visas.

We now leave Pakistan and ... for some Iranian port in the Persian Gulf. It may be Bushire or Bunder Abbas. From there we will cycle up to Teheran in March. From Teheran we go to Jordon, Lebanon and Turkey. We enter Europe through Istanbul.

Another problem for tourists like us is that of food. So far we had no difficulty about food. We got it either from the hospitable people or we bought it from the crude hotels that exist all along the main route. These hotels are used mostly by the truck drivers who move along the highways day and night. We must say that if Pakistanis want to have more and more foreign tourists like us, they must improve the sanitary conditions that exist in such hotels today.

Lastly we must say that the relations between the two neighbour countries of India and Pakistan, are to be improved by the common man of the respective countries. We will not have to wait long for a peaceful settlement of the issues, for we have found 'the man in the street' full of goodwill and understanding. Let us hope for a friendlier picture. Here, on behalf of our countrymen we take an opportunity to invite the youth of Pakistan ... India to find the facts for himself.

END

The Bharati cyclists who passed to pakistan on their way to Europe seen from left to right Mr. Ishaq Baluch, Mr. Om Prakash and Mr. S. B. Kotwal

He informed me that his trucks run between Sukkur and Hyderabad. The last truck in which I was supposed to get a lift was not yet ready. As a consolation the owner of the company invited me for the evening meal in one of the restaurants. In the meantime the truck was ready to move on. I put my bicycle and the bags on the truck and we were on the road again. We had hardly passed the bridge when there was a cracking sound and the truck bent to one side, the springs gave away due to overload. The driver took my bicycle and went back to get the necessary spare parts. It was about 03.00 a.m. when he came back with the spare parts. After about an hour we started from there and reached Hyderabad late afternoon.

Here Nana and Ishaq were waiting for me. Since we were delayed due to the breakdown the manager of the same company in Hyderabad managed so that the same trucks gave us a lift up to Karachi. Early in the morning before the sun appeared at the horizon we reached Malir (outskirts of Karachi). We slept in a restaurant and after the daybreak we cycled up to the main city. On the 19th January 1955 (83 days after the start in Poona) we reached Karachi.

Karachi

In Karachi we were put up at the old friend of Ishaqs family Mr. Jud, an English gentleman who lived alone in a bungalow in Karachi and had enough place to accommodate all three of us. Next day we reported to the police authorities thereafter we visited the offices of the news papers. Of course they were very much interested about the aim and the details of our journey. As usual there were many questions which we answered satisfactorily.

Two days after our arrival in Karachi we visited the Indian Embassy. They already knew about our venture through the news papers. The high commissioner of India in Karachi promised to help us for obtaining the visas of the countries we intended to visit on our tour. The next day we

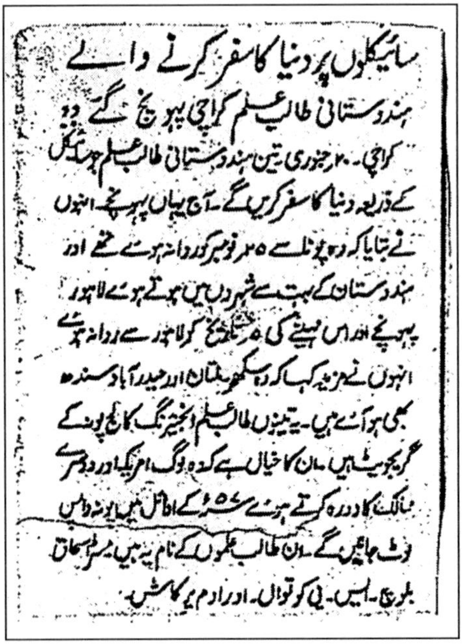
سائیکلوں پر دنیا کا سفر کرنے والے
ہندوستانی طالب علم کراچی پہونچ گئے
کراچی۔ ۲۰ جنوری تین ہندوستانی طالب علم جو سائیکل
کے ذریعہ دنیا کا سفر کریں گے۔ آج یہاں پہونچے۔ انہوں
نے بتایا کہ وہ پونا سے ۵ نومبر کو روانہ ہوئے تھے اور
ہندوستان کے بہت سے شہروں میں ہوتے ہوئے لاہور
پہونچے اور اس مہینے کی ۵ تاریخ کو لاہور سے روانہ ہوئے
انہوں نے مزید کہا کہ وہ بلوچستان اور حیدرآباد سندھ
بھی ہو آئے ہیں۔ یہ تینوں طالب علم انجینئرنگ کالج پونا کے
گریجویٹ ہیں۔ ان کا خیال ہے کہ وہ لوگ امریکا اور دوسرے
ممالک کا دورہ کرتے ہوئے ۵۸ء کے اوائل میں پونا واپس
لوٹ جائیں گے۔ ان طالب علموں کے نام یہ ہیں۔ مسٹر اسحاق
بلوچ۔ ایس۔ پی کوتوال۔ اور رادم پرکاش۔

were handed over a letter of recommendation from the office of the Indian high commissioner to be handed over to the foreign embassies with the application forms for visas. Mr. Melkani of the Indian Consular department accompanied us to the embassy of Iran in his car. On arrival we handed over to him all the necessary documents and forms for the visa. The consul of Iran promised to issue the visa within a day.

It was a great feeling to receive the visa the next day and as promised gratis by the consul of Iran. We now hoped that the representatives of other countries shall follow the example set by the embassy of Iran. In the next days we visited the embassies of Iraq, Jordan, Syria, Lebanon and Turkey to get visas. Except Turkey all the aforesaid representatives issued visas free of charge.

26th January: It was the republic day of India. We were invited by the high commissioner of India for the celebration of the day. We had now the opportunity for the second time to attend the celebration in our national costumes. At first we had planned to go by bicycles to the high commissioners premises where the celebration should take place, but then Mr. Jud encouraged us to take the bus. On arrival we were introduced to the consulates of Japan and Belgium. Both the consulates showed a great interest for our venture. It was pretty late when we realised that practically most of the invited guests had already left. We requested the attaché of the high commissioner, Mr. Mehta if he could arrange for a transport to our residence, which was gladly done.

The next two days we were busy meeting the journalists of the news papers »Dawn« and »Times«. Also lot of photographs were made by the press photographs.

On 2nd February we were invited by the Pakistan radio for an interview. Here we met Mr. Jellani who was responsible for the interview. First a test was made and then the interview was recorded to be transmitted at a later date. We were still in Pakistan when friends and family members mentioned that our interview had been »on air«.

Next day was a very important day for me personally. A day before we had visited B. I. and Pan Islamic navigation companies with the intention to find out as to what chances we had to get a free lift on a ship to Busher in Iran. The person responsible was not present. We were asked to come again the next day. In the meantime we had a great luck to obtain a reference letter to support our intention. The person in charge promised to take the ultimate decision in the next days. We came back to our residence and spent the time writing letters to relatives back home.

In the evening Ishaq opened to me that he wished to travel further alone and asked Nana about his opinion. Nana declared that he would like to travel with Ishaq further, in case Ishaq had no objections. It looked as if I was not welcome. Obviously it made me very sad, though we both Ishaq and myself had planned the whole journey together, he did not care to declare any reason for his decision. Anyhow this was the moment when I realised that three persons together is really not a good number. I could not sleep all the night. At first I felt it a very nasty and unjust step without any chance to adjust oneself to the new situation, but then regarded this as a challenge for myself.

Next morning when I got up I behaved as if I was not at all impressed by this new situation. I agreed to the decision but wished to accompany up to Persepolis in Iran and then we could go on separately. After breakfast, I went to the State Bank of India to change some money and then to the newspaper agents of »Pakistan Standard«, where they paid me Rupees 25,- for my article in their newspaper. Also some photographs were taken. In the evening I started studying the route I intended to follow carefully.

Mr. Ahesan and Mr. Farooq looked after us during our stay in Karachi and through them we got acquainted with a large number of people.

The 9th February was a day full of activities. After the breakfast we wanted to visit the information officer to find out about our chances for a lift on a ship. Since the bicycle of Nana was punctured we went by foot. The officer could not decide because the person he wished to consult was not in. He asked us to come again on the 11th February. Ishaq and myself then visited the Indian embassy, there we met a group of people from India on a good will mission to Pakistan. After they came to know about our tour and about the meagre funds that each of us had to our disposal, had the impression that we were now stuck up in Karachi. The head of the mission asked us to reconsider about our tour and should return to India. We then came back to our residence and wrote couple of letters to friends and relatives back home. Since from now on I had to travel alone I started planning for the further journey.

The first step was to buy a camera. The optical dealer had heard about us over »Pakistan Radio« so he offered me a good reduction for the camera. Also I bought few road maps. In the evening we were invited by the president of the constitutional assembly of Pakistan, Mr. Ismail. He was very courteous and mentioned that he was planning to visit some cities in the middle east, Inshaallah we may meet somewhere.

Next day we were expecting the decision for the passage by the ship to Bushehr. The decision was to be taken by the general manager of B.I. company. Our aim was to get a free passage or when it was not possible to get a reduced passage fare. The general manager requested us to wait till the next day when the ship was due to leave for the Persian gulf, however, we should keep ourselves ready and may have to embark the ship at the last moment. It was not an affirmative answer, however, sounded like a positive hope.

The 12th February was an exciting day anyway, after the breakfast we all visited the general manager of B.I. company who had to take the decision and announced that we should contribute with a small amount and the remaining difference, the bigger part shall be paid by him personally.

He gave us a note to be handed over to the person issuing the tickets. Ishaq and Nana went to secure the tickets. The general manager, Mr. Muraj promised to meet us on board and make arrangements for our journey. I had an idea to carry the flags on my bicycle, so I went to the flag maker and got the flags reduced to be fixed on the bicycle. Also I visited the Dunlop and Kodak representatives to get their company flags from them to be fixed to the bicycle. Both the representatives gave me some amount of money for the publicity of their products.

Our host Mr. And Mrs. Jud invited us for lunch on the day of our parting. It was really a grand lunch. During the lunch we informed them about our further plans. Both of them wished us good luck and all the best for the further tour. After the lunch we packed our bags together fixed these on the cycle and then said good bye to Mr. and Mrs. Jud - our host for four weeks.

With the Ship to Bushehr

We proceeded towards the shipyard where our ship was being loaded, Farooq and other friends accompanied us to the yard. We proceeded for the custom formalities. We had just started opening our bags, when the officer came forward and said« no custom formalities for you« then we got ready to go on board. It was quite a crowd pushing forward and from all sides. However, we got on board. We could not get any place on first deck and proceeded to the next one. Just as we were settling down when we were asked to come back on shore for a medical check up. This check was over in few minutes. It was very noisy during the loading period.

At about 4.15 p.m. the gangways were removed and the ship moved slowly. Lot of waving hands and loud good bye shouting were to be heard

The shipyard in Karachi

A photograph with friends before going on board

from every corner of the ship. The ship was moving in the deep waters and the silhouette of the harbour of *Karachi* was visible dimly faraway a tower of the harbour and a turret of a mosque was visible starting fading away and then there was only water all around us.

We had a tough time in securing a place to settle down and place our bags etc. At the ship we got acquainted with few people on the ship. There was quite a movement on the ship especially when the ship stopped at any harbour on the route. The captain was kind to introduce us to some of his staff colleagues to facilitate our journey. We also met a parsi fellow by the name Sonewalla who was a hitch hiker as he called himself and wanted to attend the fairs at various places on the route. The same evening we were introduced to the manager of ships company who declared to charge us 8 Pakistan Rupees only up to Bushehr.

13th February

When we got up in the morning it was very noisy around us. There were lots of passengers getting ready to go on land at Pasni.

After the passengers had left the ship the whole deck seemed to be empty. We had now more room to move around and did not have to look after our bicycles and bags as we had been doing so far. With a relaxed feeling we took a fast nap in the afternoon.

14th February

We were having our breakfast when the port of Muskat was announced to be in sight. About half a mile from the port the ship stopped. The passengers started getting down and some of them came aboard. A group of salesman came aboard to offer luxury goods free of duty. Another group of salesman belonging to another ship came aboard to join their crew. We met two Arab teachers on board and had the chance to get acquainted with the Arabian hospitality. When we went to meet them, they asked us to sit down. We were offered some self prepared coffee in a very small glass. The coffee was very strong. Also they offered Halwa and dates. We met a Syrian fellow on board who was going to Dubai and gave us lot of addresses in Damascus and other places in Syria where we could stay with their friends. In the evening we had dinner with the assistant of the captain and during the dinner we discussed about smuggling and the chances of working in Pakistan and India. We thanked the assistant captain and took leave. With all these impressions we went to sleep. At about midnight we entered the Persian Gulf.

15th February

The dawn found us near Dubai. This morning about three hundreds Arabs came aboard. The places we were occupying were taken over by them. We could not do anything against such a big number. When we tried to explain to them they would pretend not to understand us. The night was rather cool and it was not advisable to sleep on board so we decided to sleep on the top deck with little cover above.

The Arabs had a company of women, the men tried to flatter the women by offering them lot of fruits etc. Later on it turned out that the women were prostitutes and therefore practically everybody tried to flatter them with small presents. All the same it was interesting to watch them.

16th February

In the morning we reached Baharain. About 200 passengers got down here and the ship was practically empty. As a consequence of this new situation the top deck was locked. We had to leave this place and come down to the lower deck. Ishaq and Nana were trying to get a transit visa to go on shore to buy few things, like camera etc. such articles were cheaper in Baharain because there was no custom duty on such items. Both of them got the visa. Now they came to know that the boat fare for going on shore was high. The captain of our ship ultimately came to their rescue and took them in his boat. I did not accompany them and remained on the ship. I took my meals and arranged my luggage. Late afternoon all the passengers including Ishaq and Nana came back. Nana had bought a 35 mm camera.

During my trip on the ship I met Mr. Pille, the mail collector for shore, who was kind to take my letters for home, which I had written during the time Ishaq and Nana were on shore. Mr. Pille promised to post these letters personally.

I was sitting on the railing side and watching the waves in the sea and there was a light sadness in my mind because the next day we should land in Bushehr and after visiting Shiraz and Persipolis we should separate. But then the hope of making personal experiences came to my mind and I felt a bit strong in my feelings. In order not to get such thoughts I went to play table-tennis with the members of the crew. After the meals we were in search of a place to sleep, because the top deck was now closed and all the passengers were now on the second deck, which was totally crowded with passengers. I started preparing a bed on a bench, when an old woman probably the governess of the girls objected to my sleeping there, because there were young girls sleeping little further up. We then all went to the last deck and went to sleep.

Middle East

Persia

WE REACHED BUSHEHR. THE SHIP STOPPED ABOUT 500 METERS FROM THE SHORE DUE TO SHALLOW WATERS. The doctor on board was kind to give us Peludrine pills in case we needed them and wished us good luck for the further journey. The cargo was being unloaded the launch of the company had not yet arrived. While we were waiting on the deck a man asked us whether we wanted to change some money. All three of us changed some money. In the meantime the launch had arrived. We placed our luggage inside and also got a place to sit down. The launch moved towards the shore. Hardly we had moved 60 meters when the launch owner demanded the money for the fare, we hesitated first but then few passengers who came to know us on board came forward and paid for our fare.

After landing on shore we were asked to come to the police station. We had to hand over our passports. After the police authorities had examined the necessary entries in the passport, they requested us to leave our passports along with a photograph with them, so that an identity card in Persian language could be prepared. This was necessary because all the

The first inivitation after arrival in Busher

policemen posted on the border of towns could not read English. During this check up period we were served with tea and some snacks. Thereafter they asked us to make ourselves comfortable in the tourist rest house, where we shall get our passports later on. Our arrival went round like a rumour around. In the evening we were invited by the president of the education department of Iran for tea. The same afternoon the manager of the Iran national bank, Mr. Yazdani invited us to be his guest, where also the president of the education department joined us. We remained there for few hours explaining our host and other guests the aim of our tour. I was helping in replying the questions in the Persian language when necessary. We passed a pleasant time.

Late in the evening we returned to the rest house. After arrival in the rest house we were informed that a policeman had been there twice to hand us over the documents but we were not there. We were quite worried about the documents because the next day was a holiday. Our friends in the rest house then arranged over telephone such that a policeman would bring our passports the next day and then we could proceed further.

Next morning we got up early, hurriedly took our breakfast and then started cleaning our bicycles. The policeman came at 10.00 a.m. and handed over to us the passports and the identity cards. With a good bye to our hosts and friends we proceeded towards Shiraz via Borazjan and Kazerun.

Our first destination Borazjan was about 90 kilometres from Bushehr. The roads were macadamised throughout. We were a bit afraid that some puncture could occur. We were lucky to get a lift by a passing by oil truck up to about 30 kilometers from the town. Thereafter we cycled up and late in the evening reached the outskirts of the town, when a policeman stopped us and asked for the documents we handed over to him the identity card, which was prepared for this purpose in Bushehr. We were told by the authorities that practically every small village or town had city border police stationed at the outskirts of the town occupied day and night. We stayed overnight at the student hostel with the students, this way we had the opportunity to exchange the views with the students. I personally was favoured because I was well versed in Persian language and could help as interpreter if needed.

The roads in Iran

The officer apologises for the inconveniencies and brought us half the distance to the next town with the Jeep

The next day we started further to Shiraz. When we reached Kazerun the policeman stationed at the outskirts would not let us out of the city, because he could not read or write. So we were stuck up there till an officer came and realised the mishap and put a jeep to our disposal so that we could be transported to the next small village from where we cycled up to Shiraz. Late afternoon we reached Shiraz and after enquiring reached the students hostel. Here we were looked after by Mr. Mirabedy, the head of

A meeting with the students in Shiraz - In the company of the students and two tourists from France and Switzerland

the students union. They put us up in a hotel together with two hitch hikers, one from France and the other one a Swiss. They were hitch hiking to India. We all remained in Shiraz for three days and were the guest of the director of the Shiraz university. We had the chance to meet a lot of students, where we had the possibility to give a short review and aim of our journey and tried to answer possibly most of the questions put to us.

With a group of students we visited the tombs of the Poets Saadi and Hafiz, the Quran Gate, built about 1000 years ago and it is believed that in order to dispel the evil-eye from the city, a Quran was kept on it. Furthermore Vakil Mosque, Vakil Bazaar and the gardens of Shiraz, where we walked through a lane of Cyprus trees. There we all looked like a point when we passed through the lane of these trees.

The evening was my last evening with Ishaq and Nana. I remember saying to Ishaq and Nana »The earth is round, maybe we shall meet somewhere again«.

The next morning Ishaq and Nana proceeded further to Persepolis and I remained an additional day with one of the students in Shiraz. I visited the ruins of Persepolis alone. Persepolis is located 40 kilometers from Shiraz and symbolises the gigantic Persian Empire of ancient times. Persepolis lies in the shadow of the mountain Mercy. In the persian language is called »Takhate Jamshid« the throne of Jamshid semi legendary king of persia. At Persepolis I saw the ruins of the royal court, audience hall, reception rooms and quarters for foreign visitors during ceremonies. The residential palace of the king, the queen, crown prince and the royal household, administrative buildings and offices, treasury and stables.

Cypress trees in a park in Shiraz

The Apadana palace was built by Darius. The roof of the hall with Darius private palace was supported by 72 slender and graceful pillers, of which 13 still stand. The central palace was »The Council Hall« the classical name being Tripylon. The carvings on the walls of the steps depict Persian and Median officers. On the mausoleum of the great king are engraved the words:

Apadana palace in Persipolis

»O man, whatever Thou art, and where so ever Thou Cometh, For I know Thou will come, I am

Persian and Median officers on the wall

A view of the palace with Persian officers

Cyrus, who founded the Empire of the Persians. Grudge Me Not. Therefore, This little Earth That Covers My Body.«

It was my last evening. Next morning I fixed my bags on the bicycle and returned to Shiraz and after a short rest and meals at a small restaurant proceeded back towards Kazerun. Late in the evening I reached Kazerun. I had no trouble with the police stationed at the outskirts of the city. Here a Persian fellow asked me to be his guest and took me to his residence. He seemed to be working in the city office. We took this opportunity to exchange our views. Since I had cycled up all the day and was tired I went to sleep. Next morning after the breakfast consisting of goats milk and bread and eggs. I thanked my host and was again on the road towards Borazjan. I reached the city in the afternoon and had to eat whatever I was carrying because it was a Friday, that means Sunday for the people. The city seemed to be empty, therefore I thought to proceed on towards Bushehr. When I came on the outskirts of the city, I was asked to show my passport and the identity card. The policeman took the papers in the hand and turned it round and round. Now I realised that the policeman could not read or write.

The policeman would not let me go and asked me to follow him to the main police station. Here he escorted me to a well furnished room with carpets etc. It looked like an office of the officer in charge. He then gave me to understand that I had to wait till the officer in charge came back. I had no other choice than to be the guest of his majesty. Since it was friday no officer was in sight. Somewhere deep in my mind I had the feeling that the room I was waiting in should be my shelter for the night. After sometime the policeman came back and handed over to me some bread and some onion as the evening food. I had to accept the situation and thought to make the best of it. I opened my sleeping bag and went to sleep.

Next morning when the officer in charge came and saw me he apologised many times and as a compensation for the inconveniences incurred to me offered that a jeep should carry me with the cycle and bags half the way to Bushehr I accepted the offer. In about two hours the policeman left me half way to Bushehr. I now cycled up further and reached Bushehr late in the evening. The policeman at the outskirts of the city was surprised to see me. Two teachers of the school residing next to the rest house asked me to be their guests. My plan was to get a ship to Abadan and then to proceed to Iraq. I had to wait for three days in Bushehr before I could contact and request the captain of the oil ship to allow me to travel by his ship to Abadan. During my stay in Bushehr I was requested by the teachers if I would like to give a short review of the journey before the students in the school in the Persian language and answer the questions put by the students. I agreed to do that and this way made lot of friends.

1st March 1955

It was my last day in Bushehr. I thanked the two teachers and some of the students, who were accompanying me during these three days, packed my things and cycled up to the place where a boat would take me

In the company of the captain of the ship to Abadan

With the sailor on the ship to Abadan

to the oil ship ready to leave for Abadan. I said good bye to all the friends and got on the ship. The captain asked a member of the crew to accommodate me in one of the cabins. Here again the Persian language helped me and very shortly I made friends on the ship. The captain asked me to join him for the dinner where a friend of the captain was also present. It was a very nice atmosphere. Next day in the afternoon we reached Abadan. I thanked the captain and his companion and left the ship.

After landing I inquired about the address of the Roman Catholic church where I hoped to stay for the night, as such the address was given to me by the two students from France and Switzerland back in Shiraz. They had left their tent with the Rev. Francis Mulligan in Abadan. When I reached there the Bishop wanted to hand me over the tent but I requested him to keep it with him and asked him the possibility to stay for overnight. He regretted that he had no place free for me.

I came back to the city and here I met the local champion of cycling. He had already read about me in the newspapers and was glad to have me as his guest. He showed me round Abadan. A typical city with a very large oil refinery and industry. In the evening I had a chance to play hockey in the team of oil company. The other players - mostly Iranians - were pleased to have me in their team for that evening. The following days were exciting. Meeting people and giving reviews of my journey before the students in the school and club of the oil company. I remained in Abadan for five days.

In the morning I proceeded to Khorramshahr, the border city of Iran and further to the Iraq border.

Iraq

My entrance into the Iraq border was remarkable because I was asked to go back to Khorramshahr to secure the exit stamp in my passport. The officer at the Iraq border was kind to arrange a taxi which took me back to the Iran border. The officer at the Iraq border had asked the taxi driver to bring me back but I preferred to hitch hike back. After returning to the Iraq border I thanked the officer and then started towards the next town in Iraq.

The road had a broad track in sand. I followed it. After some distance more tracks appeared I was a bit confused but then decided to follow one track. After travelling for half an hour I realised that I had just gone round and had reached the starting point. Then the idea struck me to follow the telephone masts and at last late in the evening reached the border station.

Here I had the opportunity to experience the famous hospitality observed by Arabs, though I later on found out that such hospitality is practised in small villages or by nomadic Arabs. A plate full of dates, a glass of buttermilk was served as a greeting ceremony. As I was hungry I enjoyed the contents of the plate. Then I was shown round the Oasis in this small border station. After returning they served as an appetiser some-

Iraqui border guards

Children of the guards

thing which consisted of egg, bread and tea. After a gap of 15 minutes the main dinner was served. My host the border guards observed their traditions as is done by the nomadic arabs.

Next morning I thanked the border guards and cycled towards Basra and very soon reached my destination. Here I had to cross the river but had no Rials (Currency of Iraq) with me. Just then the men from the border arrived to take the food stock from the city. When they saw my difficulties, they came forward and paid the fare to the boatsman. After the fairy had reached the other side of the river I collected my bags and bicycle and cycled up towards the city. I was informed that in Basra there was an office of the Indian consulate so I proceeded for it. When I reached the consulate office I was shown in to the clerk working there. He was very rude to me. Upon my insistence to see the council I was shown in. The council got interested about my plans and was pleased to meet me. Nevertheless he did not discuss any further and went into his office. I then requested the clerk in the consulate to give me the address of the hostel of the school in the city. He did not help me. I then requested him to allow me to keep my bags in the consulate which I shall pick up later on. He allowed it.

I cycled up to the school and then tried to find out the hostel of the school. I met the person in charge of the hostel but he could not decide for my stay there and sent me to the house of the director of education. The director was not in and the deputy would not decide. I then decided to see the city and had some food in a small restaurant. I was informed that there existed an Indian rest house for tourists who come to Basra. The manager of the rest house told me frankly that the rest house was reserved for persons who come for pilgrimage to Iraq and would not accept me as such one. I was very much disgusted and remembered the night before where I had enjoyed a grand hospitality. I returned to the house of the consulate who had gone out for lunch with the American consulate. I requested his house servant to give me some place to deposit my bags, this facilitated me to visit the city by bicycle with the intention that I may meet someone who could help me. The servant was a nice fellow and allowed me to place my bags etc. in a room there.

I made two to three rounds of the city and then decided to get my hairs cut. I approached the next barber shop and asked him whether I could get a reduction being a tourist on cycle, first of all he did not agree but then I found out that he was from Iran and talked with him in Persian language. He was very pleased and agreed to take half the price. Two young men were the witness of our discussion at the barbers shop and got interested in the conversation and enquired about my future plans. They invited me to show the city and thereafter introduced me to Ali Hassan, the champion in cycle races in Basra.

Ali Hassan was interested that I should at least spend some time in Basra. He then arranged a bed for me in a hotel. In the evening I went to the house of the consulate and collected my bags and placed them at Ali Hassan's shop. Then we all went to the Bazaar and had a nice feed. During this short time I was introduced to many friends of Ali Hassan. During our visit to the Bazaar I saw a jacket in a shop and thought to buy it. Ali Hassan noticed from my views and went into the shop and talked to the merchant and after a long haggling bought the jacket for two Dinars only. I knew then that probably I would have paid the price the merchant would have demanded from me and was very pleased for this bargain.

Late afternoon Ali Hassan announced that the next day his friend was getting married and all the friends were invited and asked me to accompany him and see how Arabic marriage takes place. Obviously I was very keen to learn the Arabian traditions of marriage. In the evening we all went to attend the marriage, unfortunately the marriage ceremony was practically over when we arrived now it was the term of musicians to show their art. During the music with the drums soft drinks were passed round. At about 12.00 p.m. we wished the new wedded couple all the best in life and parted.

It appeared like a dream: In the morning when I entered Basra everything looked gloomy and in the evening it looked like a dream of reality. In the hotel I had to share the room with two persons, one was a businessman and the other one was a singer. The businessman gave me his address in Amman and invited me to see him when I would be there. The singer had somewhat paralysed hands and legs. He had travelled to Kuwait, Bombay and so on. Next morning I left them and came to Ali Hassan´s shop. Here I met further friends of Hassan. I then searched for a tailors shop to get the pockets of the jacket enlarged so that passports and other documents fit therein.

After the lunch I started cleaning my bicycle. In order to get used to some conversation words in Arabic I decided to buy an Arabic book and a road map of the middle east. One of the friends of Ali Hassan accompanied me to the bazaar. Here I could secure a book in Arabic for beginners and the required map. The time passed away very soon. Ali Hassan proposed that I should not travel to Baghdad by road as the season was awful and advised to travel by train. As a surprise he opened to me that he had already secured a ticket for me and asked me to get ready soon so that we could catch the train scheduled to leave for Baghdad in about two and a half hours time. I was overwhelmed by this grand gesture of Ali Hassan and started packing my bags together.

Before going to railway station I was introduced to the richest person of Basra. He took a keen interest in sports and after hearing about my venture was mighty impressed and asked me to get a pamphlet printed which should serve as an introduction to the public, press and otherwise. He handed over to me ten Dinars as his contribution for the further journey. The time being very short we rushed up to the railway station. Ali Hassan, who was famous for cycle acrobatics took a ride standing upright on the fixing nuts of the rear wheel right up to the station. On the way Ali Hassan was asking me to look after my health and advised me to get some pamphlets with my photograph and some text to present it to the people on the way. This could help me getting to know people and it would help me also financially.

We reached the railway station before I could get into the train, a policeman came forward and asked for my passport. After checking the entries in the passport he allowed us to proceed on. I then locked the bicycle and placed it into the compartment where the accompanying baggage of the passengers was deposited. Ali Hassan seemed to be very cautious and every now and then would remind me to take care of my ticket and baggage. I found a place for my baggage and also a seat for me. Now it was time to say good bye to Ali Hassan and other friends who had come to see me off. Ali Hassan would not let me go without saying me good bye the way Iraqis do. He held my head in his hands and gave me kiss on each cheek. The train started and I could see handkerchiefs in the hands waving fading far away as the train rolled on. I settled down on my seat.

The persons sitting around me offered me food, cigarettes tea etc. after they came to know about my tour. There was an old man in the compartment having something wrong with his leg. We vacated a seat for him and accommodated him there, he would cry whenever he changed his position.

In the compartment it was rather congested to accommodate all of us comfortably. My neighbour spread his blanket on the floor between the two seats and asked me whether I would like to sleep for a while. I was very much pleased for the offer and did lie down but could not sleep. After some time I asked my neighbour to exchange the place with me. This way half dosing away we continued on. The train stopped practically at every station on the route, some people would get down and others would get into the compartment.

The dawn was announced by a cock accompanying us in the compartment and soon it was bright daylight everywhere.

The train reached Baghdad at 10.30 a.m. I took my bicycle from the baggage compartment and fixed my bags on it and cycled up towards the Indian embassy. After some difficulty I was successful in finding it. In the embassy they were pleased to see me, as such they had already read about my venture in the newspaper. They arranged to send me to the Indian association, where I was welcomed by Mr. Sharma who looked after the Indian community residing in Baghdad. The next day I tried to meet the ambassador of India in Iraq but he was out of Iraq so I met the 2nd secretary, Mr. Mahaboob Ahmed and for remembrance made a photograph with him. I remained in Baghdad for seven days.

In the neighbourhood of the Indian Association lived the family of Mr. Saad, who was a constant companion throughout the time I remained in Baghdad. One of the evenings we visited a boxing match in the stadium. The next day I went to the Indian embassy to meet the 2nd secretary, who was also charge de affairs. He was interested to meet me to get himself informed about my mission because he had read about me in the Iraq Times. He asked me to follow him to his room. After knowing the details of my mission he advised me to write to the director of the education requesting them to nominate me to the ministry of external affairs for further studies in Germany, which he was sure shall be supported.

I promised to do it. I asked him for the possibility of obtaining an autograph from his excellency the king Hussain. He said he could arrange for a recommendation letter but was not sure to be successful.

Then we had a photograph together as a remembrance. Mr. Mahaboob then arranged for an interview with the Iraq Broadcasting authorities. They were unable to give me a chance because I was not well versed in Arabic language. 13th March was the Holi-Festival (a Hindu festival celebrating the begin of the spring season, when people fly kites and dress up in clothes of different colours to welcome the spring season). Mr. Sharma expected members of the Indian colony in the evening. He then asked me whether I was interested to hold a review of my journey before the gathering. I regarded this as a grand opportunity to give a review of the journey before a big gathering.

During the day many people came to this prayer meeting. After Mr. Sharma had finished with the prayers, I was asked to come forward and gave a short review of my venture. After my review there was a big applause and praise for my courage. At this gathering I handed over my photograph with my signature to persons who asked for it. As their contribution and

A photograph with Mr. Sharma

Myself in Arab dress

Friends in the neighbourhood in Baghdad - Mr. Sharma and the people in the neighbourhood

assistance some Dinars were donated. They all wished me good luck for the further journey.

The next day I visited the main distributing agents of Coca Cola, Dunlop and Kodak and met their managers. They made photographs with me and gave autographs with good wishes for the further journey and of course some money for the publicity of their products. The following day I was invited by Mr. Mohinder of the British stores, who gave me a grand feed in one of the posh hotel restaurant and thereafter we both travelled by bus to Kazrun, a place where the old khalif Haroon Al-Rashid used to rule. Here was buried a prophet of Shea with a large marble area around it and a beautiful mosque in the neighbourhood. I went inside the mosque and saw around people praying, lot of them were crying. They say if you go round it once and wish something it comes true. I went round it and wished that my mission may lead to success and I may return back to India safely.

Also we saw the ornamental handicraft work. We returned back to the centre of Baghdad. I thanked my host and took my bicycle and went to the Indian embassy. Here I was introduced to Jabbar Muzafar, a stu-

"THE IRAQ TIMES", March 12, 1955.

* * *

FROM the opposite direction, on a bicycle, has come Omprakash Virmani, a graduate of Poona's College of Engineering. Starting on a world tour from Poona, he has already covered 5,500 miles, his itinerary taking him across India, through Pakistan and Iran to this country. A few days in Baghdad and he will be off again, across the desert to Amman, Jerusalem, Damascus and Beirut and then on to Turkey, Continental Europe and Britain.

Mr. Virmani proposes to spend two years in advanced studies in the field of tele-communications, either in Britain or West Germany. Afterwards he will cross the Atlantic to the United States for further studies, and retaining his cycle, will return to India by 1960.

dent who had travelled to Cairo by bicycle. He gave me some tips about the journey to Amman. He advised me to travel by bus because this distance of about 600 kilometers is a tough distance to cover since it is all desert with side winds. I was determined to cover the distance with my own efforts. We both then visited the museum and thereafter a cinema show. The manager of the cinema was kind to let me in the cinema free.

We both were just passing a gate of ministry of defence when I asked Muzafar to stand in front of this gate and took a photograph. Just the next moment the soldier on guard came forward and asked me to follow him to his office. He thought I was a foreign spy or something like that. The officer in charge was not in the office so I was asked to wait for him. After about half an hour the officer in charge came. He escorted me to the security officer, who after hearing the facts asked me if I wished to have another photograph with him. I took a photograph in presence of the soldier who had brought me into this situation. Muzaffar had already left. I came back to the association, wrote some letters home and started planning to start the next day to Amman.

The next day I got up in the morning and had a grand breakfast with my host, Mr. Sharma. Thereafter I took some photographs with him. I thanked him for the grand help and the hospitality. I told him that I had felt like at home with him and said good bye to him and to the friends living in the neighbourhood and started toward the road leading to Amman.

The police constables stationed there acted as border guards who would check all the persons and traffic moving into and going out of the city. The officer in charge told me frankly that the distance of about 560

A photograph with the officer before the gate to the defense ministry

Modern Baghdad

kilometers up to Amman was a desert with sandy side winds. Also I was informed that along the road towards Amman there were small places where one can rest for a while or find shelter for overnight. I thanked the officer and proceeded further on the road. The sun was high in the sky and it was very hot. The Australian hat I was wearing gave me some protection against the sun but the heat was unbearable.

First day I covered about 160 kilometers and stopped in a small hut alongside of the road. I took out the food I was carrying and the water bottle, ate something and tired as I was went to sleep.

Early in the morning before the sun was out far away in the horizon, I packed my bags and moved on with the intention to cover more distance than the day before. While I was on the road, a truck carrying oil and then a bus overtook me. The passengers in the bus waved to me with loud shouting. During the day more trucks overtook me. Late afternoon I saw from far away a silhouette of a truck, at first I thought it to be a fata morgana, but then as I came near, I found to my relief a real truck. The driver and the co.-driver greeted me. They had stopped to get the engine cooled, where the lid of the cooler was open and the steam streaming out. I sat down in the shade of the truck and ate some food carrying with me they offered me some water and gave me some more food for the way. I thanked both of them and after some rest carried on.

There was strong side wind and it was difficult to paddle up fast. Before the sun set I had covered about 150 kilometers and stopped in a hut alongside of the road. I was very tired and after some food went to sleep. When I woke up the dawn had set in. Hurriedly I packed my bags and moved on to cover as much distance as possible to be near to my goal. The sun was high in the sky and it was very hot with side winds, which made it very tough for me to cycle on. A truck full of load was driving slowly, it encouraged me to hold the truck and travel this way for some time. Travelling this way was obviously comfortable but also dangerous when other vehicles overtook the truck. I travelled this way for about 15 kilometers and then started paddling on my own. Late in the evening I reached a control post for the trucks and decided to stop there for the night. This day I had covered about 150 kilometers. Next morning when I got up my muscles were stiff because of the cold at night. I then decided to take a bus for the last 140 kilometers to Amman.

Jordan

In the afternoon I reached Amman. The Consulate Office at Baghdad had informed me that Mr. Mirchandani, who owned an Indian antiquarian shop also looked after the interests of the Indian government as honorary counsel, and that I should visit while I was in Amman. After reaching the bus station in Amman I asked the policeman guiding the traffic about the location of the shop and then asked him whether I could have a photograph with him. Upon his agreement I requested a person on the road to take a photograph. With this gesture the policeman was so impressed that he left the traffic guiding circle and guided me straight to the said shop and after shaking hands wished me good luck and left. I entered the shop and introduced myself to Mr. Mirchandani. He after hearing my story in short asked me to keep my bags, sleeping bag etc. in his shop and invited me to join him for the lunch.

Photograph with the policeman guiding the traffic

During the lunch Mr. Mirchandani told me that he was living in Amman for the last 20 years. When he came to Amman from Baghdad for business, shaik Abdullah was the ruler. At the shop of Mr. Mirchandani I was introduced to Mr. Diwan, first secretary to the Ambassador of India in Baghdad, who was touring around. and was to leave for Damascus. During our conversation it turned out that he knew our family back home very well. He was pleased to meet me and wished me good luck for the further journey.

During my stay in Amman I met a boy living next door to the shop and invited me to visit his family. His sister asked me into the house, she introduced me to her parents and her elder sister, who was divorced, this I came to know later on. This was my first acquaintance with a Greek family. They had read about my venture and naturally were interested to know about myself and obviously about India etc.

After about one and a half hours of stay I left with the promise to come again and returned to the shop. Mr. Mirchandani asked me to accompany him to his house. He introduced me to his wife. My first impression was that she could be categorised as a modern woman, as such during my stay with them I noticed that she did not mind to smoke or drink when she found herself in a good society, however all the time I was their guest I did not see her either drinking or smoking.

Jerusalem

I informed my host that I intended to pay a short visit to Jerusalem the next day. Next morning after having my breakfast I accompanied Mr. Mirchandani to his shop to collect the sleeping bag, a pyjama, the bicycle and the tools for the journey, and then took leave from my host and started for Jerusalem.

In the beginning the road had few steep climbings but I carried on and reached the village Suweilih. The countryside is really beautiful and everywhere it was green. The Cyprus trees make the landscape very beautiful and enchanting. After Suweilih the road had many steep ups and downs I asked the driver of a truck passing by whether he would give me a lift. He refused to do it but allowed me to hold the truck. This way I reached the climb. Then the road lead downwards right up to Jericho. The landscape all around was green and pleasant to the eyes.

At Jericho I managed to get the lunch together with the assistance of a student, who accompanied me to the shop and translated the items in Arabic. In the meantime the people had gathered around me because the student had told them about me. A policeman came and greeted me and asked the people to leave me alone. After the lunch I proceeded further. I was advised by the people to take a bus than to travel by bicycle, because the road ahead had very steep climbing. I intended to go on further by bicycle and therefore continued on. Since it was very hot in the sun I was sweating and feeling tired.

24—3—55

JERUSALEM THURSDAY

يطوف العالم على دراجة

زارنا في ادارة هذه الجريدة امس الطالب الهندي امبراكاش فيرماني الذي يقوم بجولة علمية حول العالم على دراجته « بسكليت »

وقد غادر السيد فيرماني بلدته « بونا » في الهند في ٢٨ تشرين الاول من العام الماضي على دراجته الى مدينة دلهي ومنها الى كشمير فلاهور وكراتشي ، حيث ركب الى بيشاور في ايران احدى البواخر ثم سافر الى اصفهان وعبدان ومنها الى القطر العراقي حيث زار البصرة وبغداد واستانف سيره الى الجفور ، وهنا بدات الامطار بالهطول فاستقل سيارة الى المفرق حيث ركب سيارته الى الى عمان فالقدس .

وابلغنا الطالب المذكور انه يستعد الان للسفر على دراجته الى دمشق ومنها مخترقا اوروبا الي المانيا حيث يقضي سنتين في احدى الجامعات وبعد ذلك يذهب الي اميركا حيث يمكث فترة من الزمن يكمل فيها تعليمه العالي ثم ينتقل بعدئذ الى الشرق الاقصى لزيارة الصين واليابان ثم يعود الى الهند .

Late in the afternoon I reached a place about 23 kilometers before Jerusalem. Here I went inside a restaurant alongside of the road and asked for water. In a very short moment a rumour went round the restaurant „yahudi yahudi“ it meant a Jew, a Jew. Everybody looked at me suspiciously soon there was a big gathering around me, my forehead was wet and my face showed fear. Just then a well dressed person, who probably realised the situation came forward and asked about my nationality. When I showed him my passport he told around in the restaurant about my identity. All of a sudden the tension in the restaurant turned into friendly words offering me food, tea etc. The well dressed person turned out to be a journalist working for Jordan newspaper called »Al Jordan«. He invited me to visit him while I was in Jerusalem and promised to bring my story in the newspaper. I was given a grand see off from the guests in the restaurant. The way further on was very tough. I had to walk up few kilometers towing the bicycle.

Late in the evening I reached Jerusalem. Here I inquired about the Indian hospice, where all the Indian tourists resided when they visit the holy city. In the hospice I could occupy a room and since I was very tired and had headache due to the strong heat by the shining sun all the time. I got into my sleeping bag without changing my clothes and without eating anything and went to sleep. I do not know how long I had been sleeping, when I heard a knock on the door and the attendant of the hospice accompanied with a bearded person entered the room. He introduced himself to me. He was the headmaster of a school in Burma and was on his way to visit all the holy places. He offered me some Indian sweats and fruits. After we had exchanged our identities we agreed to go round together to visit the historical places in the city the next day.

The old city of Jerusalem (in Arabic: El Kuds) is covered by a four kilometer city wall including 34 turrets and 8 towers. The city covers 4 areas, the Christian area, the Jewish area, the Moslem area and the Armenians area and many museums and churches. Mr Maulana, that was the person from Burma and myself started the next day for a visit to the Mosque of Omar. While we were entering the old city, a young man hoping to earn some money guided us first to the church where Christ was crucified, a rock cracked into two pieces. They say this rock got cracked when the soul of Christ left his body. Then the place where he was washed. And then the tomb where he was buried with a removed stone, which they say was removed by the angel on the second day. The church is supported by large iron supporters against earthquake shocks

We proceeded towards Omars mosque, where they say that prophet Mohamad was brought from Madina and prayed in the

The Mosque of Omar

The church of the holy Sepulehre

A visit to Bethlehem birthplace of Christ

At the hospice in Jerusalem after arrival

mosque Aqsa and then rode up towards heaven. Mr. Maulana remained in the mosque with the intention to pray and remain there till late in the evening. Due to the tension between Arabs and Jews the programme ended by 8.30 p.m., because in the evening the gun shots were exchanged across the divided city with barbed wire and the lights were dimmed or switched off. On the way back to the hospice I met a family from Iran whom I had been helpful to find their hotel. Since I had been in Iran and quite versed in Persian language, they invited me for a dinner in the hotel. I did not want to offend the host and joined them for the dinner. After the food I returned to the hospice and went to sleep.

The next day Mr. Maulana and myself decided to visit Hebron, where prophet Abraham, Yusuf and Ishaq are buried. We took a bus. The road was full of serpentines. Fortunately I hadn't taken my breakfast and Mr. Maulana was fasting on that day, so that I was lucky not to face inconveniences if the stomach had been full. On arrival in Hebron a guide looked after us but when he came to know that I

الاردن

الجمعه
٢٥ اذار سنة ١٩٥٥ م
١ شعبان سنة ١٣٧٤ ه
العدد ٣١١٧

وصول سائح هندي

على دراجة يطوف بها العالم

عمان – وصل الى العاصمة امس السائح الهندي السيد اومبركاش ورماني قادما من الهند على دراجة عادية وهو يقوم برحلة حول العالم على دراجته وقد ترك بومباي يوم ٢٨ تشرين اول سنة ١٩٥٤ وقد مر بدلهي وكشمير وباكستان وايران والعراق ووصل الى الاردن

وزار القدس وبيت لحم والخليل ورام الله وسيترك عمان الى دمشق فبيروت فتركيا ومنها الى اوروبا

وهو متخصص في (راديو تلفيجن) وفي الرادار واللاسلكي والتلفون والتلغراف

وسيبقى في المانيا سنتين للاستزادة من فنه ثم يزور فرنسا فبريطانيا ومنها الى اميركا فاليابان فالصين فالهند عائدا الى بلده

was non-Muslim, I was not allowed to enter the mosque. I sat outside and consoled myself saying that god is everywhere. We returned back to Jerusalem.

Next day I was invited by the journalist of »Al diffa« for an interview. The brother of the director of the newspaper was not present so his younger brother interviewed me and heard about my venture and was impressed. He then took a photograph of me and promised to send me a copy of the interview and a copy of the newspaper c/o Indian Embassy in Damascus. As his contribution he handed over to me an envelope with some Dinars in it for the further journey. I came back to the hospice. In the evening together with a fellow, whom I used to meet daily he went through the old city of Jerusalem for the last time. We had nice Kebabs and bread together and enjoyed the evening.

It was the parting day. First of all I thought to travel by bus, but then I decided to find out whether it was possible to read a newspaper while lying on the back in the dead sea water. I parted from my hosts of the hospice and was again on the road to Jericho. The road to Jericho was all along down hill and made the travelling much easier. I reached my destination after about one and half hour. From Jericho I cycled up to the Dead Sea. It was afternoon time there were hardly anybody around except two persons, who were basking in the sun after a bath in the sea. The cabins for changing the clothes or showers after the bath in the sea were locked. I just took off my clothes behind one of these cabins and with my under wear went into the water and tried to lie down on my back in the water. It is true one does not get drowned. I remained in the water for about half an hour. After this experience I got out of the water and wished to have a shower. Unfortunately I had no chance at all. I just dressed up with clumsy feeling with all the salt sticking on my body. I cycled up to the road to Jericho and then to proceed further to Amman. Since my body was full of salt I was sweating terribly. I then decided to take a bus ride from Jericho to Amman.

At the bus station the ticket conductor, who was waiting for the bus saw me and became inquisitive about my person and asked me all the possible questions. He seemed to be impressed after he came to know about my mission and handed over to me a gratis ticket to travel by bus to Amman. After an hours journey I was again in Amman.

After arrival I went straight to the shop of my host, Mr. Mirchandani. He asked me to wait at the shop till the evening, since his wife was visiting friends and I would not meet anybody there.While I waited at the shop Mrs. Mirchandani visited the shop and informed her husband that they were invited that evening and that she was all the time at home. I was flabbergasted about the situation because I felt very clumsy by the salt on my body and wanted to have a bath to free my body from the dead sea salt. All the same I had to wait till 7.30 p.m. when my host closed the shop and we together went home. He asked me to hurry up since they were invited. I requested him to allow me to remain at the residence so that I could take a bath and take some rest. He agreed to my request and showed me where I could have my bath and where I could prepare my evening meal.

After I was alone I leisurely shaved myself and then had a bath and also washed few clothes with the thought that I may not get another chance to wash my clothes. Thereafter I sat down and wrote few letters home and listened to the radio. At about 10.30 p.m. my host returned, we chatted a little and then we all went to sleep.

Next morning after the breakfast I joined my host to his shop, where I kept the washed clothed in the bags of my cycle. Then I accompanied him to the passport office where he had to obtain a visa for his servant, who wished to visit Iraq. He knew many people and he introduced me to business friends who visited him at the shop. He then called the Jordan Press so that they could take the details of my journey and the further plans. I went to the newspaper. An assistant journalist noted down the details, made a photograph of me and then wished me all the best for the further journey. He promised to send me a copy of the newspaper c/o Indian Embassy in Damascus. The remaining day I spent with some people whom I came to know during my stay in Amman.

I decided to leave Amman the next day to continue the journey to Damascus. The first job to be done was to get an exit stamp from the police authorities. Both myself and my host were up early. Mr. Mirchandani prepared the morning tea and handed me over one. Thereafter I went to the police station. On reaching there I found that I was the first person to enter the office which was not yet open for public. After some waiting the police officer in charge came and I could secure the stamp in my passport. I came back to the residence of my host and took a hurried breakfast. Mrs. Mirchandani offered me a double portion of eggs with the comments, I needed that to be strong for the further journey. The host handed over to me an envelope with some Dinars for the journey. I thanked my host and his wife for the great help and the hospitality offered to me during my stay with them and went with the host to his shop. After arriving there I changed my travelling clothes and said good bye to him and to the few young people with whom I had got acquainted during my stay and then parted.

At the traffic crossing I asked somebody to take a photograph of me with the policeman controlling the traffic at the crossing of the roads. On my way I saw the signboard of the newspaper »Aardun«. The journalist saw me and came running out with a copy of the newspaper in which my story was published. He handed this to me with a remark that now he need not send me a copy at the address in Damascus. I thanked him and moved on towards the border to Syria.

I was told that a new road, with a shorter distance to the border had been built which leads over **Jarash, Ar Ramtha to the Syrian border to Dara**. I followed this new road. I knew that the road up to Suwaylih covered many ups and downs. During paddling down a slope the front wheel of the bicycle struck a stone lying on the road and caused a puncture. I stopped at once to avoid bigger damage and sat down along the roadside to repair the punture. After half an hour I was again on the road. At times the climbs were so steep that I had to walk instead of cycling. By afternoon I had covered 25 kilometers. After some rest I started again, now it was easy going because the road followed downwards. I had to be careful least the breaks of the bicycle failed. After some distance I reached a bridge on a large stream of water. I was hungry and thirsty and was in search of a possibility where I could have some food.

I saw a car parked with about six persons around, I asked a person as to where I could get food. He could not understand me. Another person nicely dressed up approached me and I put him the same question. He understood English and introduced himself as a teacher in the next town. After hearing my story he at once invited me to take food with them. We both followed to the tent beside the stream and joined them. We had a grand meal with butter, eggs etc. He asked me whether I would go with him to the village which I had already passed. I apologised for not making it possible because I wanted to reach Jarash by the evening and visit the old roman city before it got dark. I thanked him for the food and cycled up towards the city. I met two persons on the road and asked them about the way to the city and about the possibility for the accommodation. They said it was too late to travel further and offered me to be their guest and sleep in a tent. I gladly accepted their offer since I was very tired. Two more persons joined us. They had blond hairs, so I named them Scotsman; they were pleased to get such a name. They prepared tea for me. After we had the tea we decided to visit the old city of Jarash, now of course ruins.

I being a special guest they let me in gratis and the guide showed us round the ruins giving details. We saw the amphitheatre, the roman church thereby he gave us the details of the architect of old time. After visiting the old city we returned to the tents. Here the head of the camp had arrived. He was very pleased to meet me. He then mentioned that the Royal Government of Jordan was not in a position to spare enough money for the maintenance of the ruins of the old city of Jarash, they received a donation of about 10.000 Guinea from British Government every year. Thereafter we had an exchange of general views since both of us were tired we decided to go to bed and soon I was fast asleep.

Next morning, after I was ready to leave, I thanked my hosts for the grand hospitality, then said good bye and rolled on towards Ar Ramtha. Since I had no more films with me I could not make any photographs of my hosts and the ancient city of Jarash. After I reached the city I asked a person about the new road towards Ar Ramtha. At first I was directed to the old road. After some distance I realised the error, returned back and then took the right road to Ar Ramtha. The road had steep climbs, I was just wondering as to how many kilometers such climbs will be when a water tank truck passed me, which supplied water to the labourers working on the road. On request he gave me a lift up to Ar Ramtha. After reaching the city of Ar Ramtha I cycled up to the border control station, where I got a stamp in my passport. After these formalities the police and custom authorities gave me a warm good bye with long shake hands and a kiss on each cheek and wished me good luck for the further journey. About 100 meters from this point were hanging two big signboards indicating the boundaries of Jordan and Syria, unfortunately I could not make a photograph of it as an alibi.

Syria

To enter the Syrian ground I had to pass through a gate, where first check up took place. The officer in charge was kind to direct me to the next building for the passport and custom control. Before going to the next post I requested the officer if he could post my letter for my elder brother which I was carrying in my pocket and had forgotten to post at Ar Ramtha. He promised to post it. Next I had to go through the custom formalities. They let me go further without opening any bags. Thereafter I entered another post in which the passports were controlled. The officer in charge put my passport ahead of others and after putting the entry stamp in my passport wished me all the best for the further journey.

A gentleman, who seemed to be a student came forward and asked me whether I could spare few moments for him. In fact he wanted to talk to me about my tour. I accepted his request. He asked me to accompany him to the restaurant, where we had some tea. My narration of the journey fascinated him so much that he invited me to be his guest for that day. I accepted the invitation and accompanied him to his residence, about four kilometers from the border in the city Dara. My stay in Dara was made very exciting and comfortable by the two students Walid and Faisel.

During this short stay I had the opportunity to meet many students and a teacher of the school, with whom I could exchange our views in English because my knowledge about French was at a lower level. There was a controversy between Walid and Faisel about the role of a host. Ultimately they agreed that I should sleep for the night at Faisels residence and have my breakfast at Walids place. In the evening more friends of Walid came to meet me. Naturally there were lot of questions about India. As such they expressed a great respect and sympathy for Jawahar lal Nehru and Mahatma Gandhi and of course the policy of non violence. We had then discussion why Hindus burn their deads and why they do not eat beef etc. I tried my best to give satisfactory arguments for the said traditions. It was late and everybody felt tired. I apologised myself, said good night and went to bed.

Next morning Faisel told me that one of their friends was leaving for Damascus and shall meet me and try to make arrangements for my stay there. We all came to Walids house and had the breakfast together. After the breakfast I changed my clothes and was ready to be on the road again. Walid, Faisel and a group of his friends escorted me to the outskirts of Dara and wished me all the best for the further journey to Damascus.

There was west wind a bit cold but good for cycling. The landscape was green. There were few steep climbs but in all it was easy going. I was about 10 kilometers from Damascus, when out of the bus passing by the friend of Walid leaned out of the window of the bus and shouted that he shall be waiting for me in the city.

Damascus

I hurried up to cover up the last 10 kilometers. In this moment these 10 kilometers appeared like 100 kilometers. At last I reached the city and joined the gentleman waiting for me. First of all we decided to visit few newspaper agencies, which we did. Since we were hungry we decided to have some food.

After the lunch in a restaurant we decided to leave the bicycle at the restaurant and to visit few friends. I was introduced to Mr. Ali. He was my host for the whole next week and arranged my stay in a hotel. During my stay in Damascus I came to know a person, who was in prison for a long time, he was very sore about the Jews. Also I was acquainted with an organisation called »Alkume Alsuria Alajeamai«, which was founded by Mr. Saada. Mr. Saada had fought for the freedom of Syria from the French occupation and was executed during the French occupation of Syria. His aim was to get Syria free from the French occupation and promoted close understanding between the Arab countries. He was dead now but the organisation kept his ideals alive and propa-

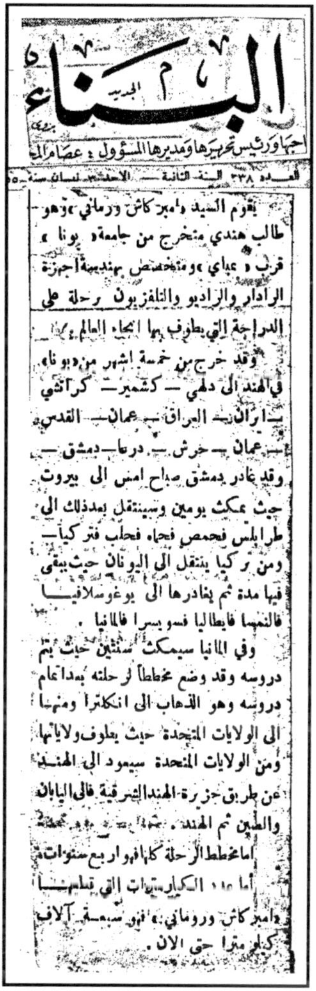

البناء الجديد

يقوم السيد «ابركاش ورماني» وهو طالب هندي متخرج من جامعة «بونا» قرب «بمباي» ومتخصص بهندسة اجهزة الرادار والراديو والتلفزيون رحلة على الدراجة التي يطوف بها انحاء العالم.

وقد خرج من خمسة اشهر من «بونا» في الهند الى دلهي — كشمير — كراتشي — ايران — العراق — عمان — القدس — عمان — جرش — درعا — دمشق — وقد غادر دمشق صباح امس الى بيروت حيث يمكث يومين وسينتقل بعد ذلك الى طرابلس فحمص فحماه فحلب فتركيا — ومن تركيا ينتقل الى اليونان حيث يبقى فيها مدة ثم يغادرها الى يوغوسلافيا فالنمسا فايطاليا فسويسرا فالمانيا.

وفي المانيا سيمكث سنتين حيث يتم دروسه وقد وضع مخططاً لرحلته بعد اتمام دروسه وهو الذهاب الى انكلترا ومنها الى الولايات المتحدة حيث يطوف ولاياتها ومن الولايات المتحدة سيعود الى الهند عن طريق جزيرة الهند الشرقية فالى اليابان والصين ثم الهند.

اما مخطط الرحلة كلها فهو اربع سنوات.

اما عدد الكيلومترات التي قطعها «ابركاش ورماني» فهو سبعة آلاف كيلومترا حتى الان.

A photograph with the minister John at the embassy in Damascus

gated its aim among the Arab people. During my stay I was taken care of by the different members of the organisation. They also published a press report in their newspaper about my journey with a photograph of mine. For this report I was paid by the newspaper. A letter of recommendation was handed over to me for their organisation in Beirut.

During my stay in Damascus I also visited the agents of the Dunlop company to get the tyres of the bicycle. The manager of the agency was a very nice gentleman, however. Since the size of the tyres used by me on my bicycle was not available he offered me fifteen Syrian pounds as a compensation so that I could buy the tyres on my way. He then got my bicycle checked in his workshop.

Since all the pages of my passport were full of entries I visited the Indian embassy a day before I was due to leave for Beirut. The consul requested me to write few words in the guest book. The same evening the minister Mr. John in the Indian embassy invited me for a lunch at his residence. During the lunch Mr. John intimated to me that he shall be leaving for Rome as ambassador of India in Italy. He wished me good luck and hoped to see us again in Rome.

Next day I was on the road again towards Beirut. At first the landscape was beautiful. After sometime the scenery changed and there was no vegetation. It became very hot. In about four hours I had covered about 40 kilometers. I was sweating and thirsty. I saw a man waiting along the roadside for a bus. Just in the next moment a bus stopped in front of us.

The driver asked me to put my bicycle in the bus. The man, with whom I had been talking turned out to be an engineer at the Damascus radio station. After coming to know that I had also graduated in the same field, he asked me whether I was interested to visit the radio station. I gladly accepted the invitation. He showed me around the medium wave transmitters with 25 kW transmitting energy and further two transmitters for short wave broadcasting.

Two persons from the group of technicians working there could converse with me in English. Lot of questions were put. It seemed that one of them had been to Bombay and praised the tea served in the Indian restaurants. During our conversation a person from the group brought a newspaper in which there was a column about me. After they had read the column they were overwhelmed about my venture and handed over 6 Syrian pounds as a contribution for my further journey. The same bus brought me back to the main road.

Once on the road, I cycled further toward Beirut. I had hardly covered half the distance to Beirut when the steep climbs started. It being very hot I was thinking either to take a lift by bus or to walk the distance up to the top of the climbing. I saw a bus approaching so I stopped it and took the ride up to the top of the climbing.

Lebanon

Beirut

Down there the skyline of the city of Beirut and far away the blue see and the shore lay before me cycling down the road was interesting but also risky. The roads were narrow and with heavy traffic. Before leaving Damascus I had written to the secretary of the Y.M.C.A in Beirut and requested them for accommodation during my stay in Beirut. I asked a person about the address of the Y.M.C.A but he did not know about it. Then I approached a young man who had the hood of his car open and was waiting when the hot steam out of the cooler has stopped. I asked him whether I could help him. He replied that he was new in Beirut and had to meet an estate agent who was going to help him find a house. In this house he intended to start the manufacturing of different furniture models of chairs and tables etc.

After he came to know my problem he requested me to put my bicycle and the bags in his car. After arriving he left these with one of his friends house and asked me to accompany him. We visited quite a number of buildings. Ultimately he decided to rent a big room in a new building. He paid a months rent to the estate agent and then we returned to his friends house. I took my bicycle and bags and we both went in search of Y.M.C.A. My host took the tram and myself along the tram. After searching for an hour we reached the premises of Y.M.C.A. The secretary was not in. But he had left a message for me that he was sorry not being able to help me and asked me to try with youth hostel association. My companion now decided that we put the baggage and the bicycle in a taxi and drive to the youth hostel. Ultimately we got there. The director after meeting me gladly gave me a room to stay. We thanked each other for the help and then parted. I was so tired from the heat that I opened my bed and went to sleep.

It was quite dark when I got up. I had not eaten since afternoon and felt very hungry. I washed myself, changed my clothes and went out. I asked a person on the road about the main bazaar. He was very helpful and accompanied me in a bus to the main bazaar and showed me round. I asked him whether he could direct me to an Indian shop, where I intended to change some money. At first he offered to give me some money but I could not accept the offer, however, he was kind to guide me to the Indian shop. I thanked him and got into the shop. Here I introduced myself to the owner and requested him to change some money. He was kind to change the money and gave me a better rate than official one.

My head was aching very much. The owner of the shop gave me an Aspirin and a Coca Cola. I came back to the hostel and just as I wanted to go to sleep when my nose started bleeding. Probably it was the heat during the whole day. I went to the bath room and poured water on my

الصرخة » — الصحية

الثلاثاء ٢٩ آذار ١٩٥٥—

سائح هندي

زار إدارة « الصرخة » بعد ظهر امس طالب هندي يقوم بجولة سياحية حول العالم على البسكليت وهو يدعى السيد « اومبرا كاش فيلوماني » وقد انهى دراسته في الهند وسيقوم باكمال هذه الدراسة بعد ان ينهي سياحته . وقد غادر نيودلهي قبل خمسة اشهر ، فزار ايران والعراق والباكستان وانكلترة على البسكليت ، ثم جاء الى عمان ومنها الى درعا ومن درعا قطع المسافة الى دمشق بخمس ساعات ، وسيقضي في دمشق يومين ثم يذهب بعدها الى لبنان ومنها الى اوربة وسيحط في آخر الامر في المانية لاتمام دراسته هناك .

head and the bleeding stopped. The room I was accommodating contained 25 beds but I was the only guest in the hostel. At night it being very hot inside I moved my bed half outside the room and went to sleep. Just before the dawn broke it became slightly cool and therefore I shifted inside the hostel.

There were quite a number of tennis courts around the hostel and slowly all the courts were occupied. A group of students heard about me and joined me in the hostel and after hearing about my venture made photographs of me and an article was published in the Armenian language. A copy of the newspaper in which a report about me was published was handed over to me by the manager of the hostel director for information.

Before I left Damascus a letter addressed to »Alkami Alsurya« was handed over to me so that the members of the organisation should be helpful to me during my stay in Beirut. I asked few people on the said address but nobody seemed to know the organisation. I asked a person who turned out to be an Egyptian. He knew a student living in the hostel, who was a member of the organisation. After a long search I found him. The young fellow introduced me to a group of students living in the student hostel. It being late in the evening he requested me to meet him again the next morning.

I was introduced to a large group of students of the university the next morning, where I was asked to give a short review and the aim of my journey, which I gladly did.

An orient bazaar.

الحياة

إن الحياة عقيدة وجهاد

AL-HAYAT No 2738 — BEYROUTH Le 7-4 1955

الرحالة الهندي اوم براماباش فيرمانو الذي وصل الى بيروت في جولته حول العالم على دراجة عادية. وقد قطع حتى الان ..٧٠٢ كيلو متر وعليه ان يجتاز ..٥٥ كيلو متر اخرى ويرى الرحالة الهندي مع دراجته امام احدى سيارات [illegible] « الحياة »

A press report in the newspaper »Al Hayat« in Beirut

They were all impressed about my venture. Next day I met Jamal Musa, a medical student in his last year of studies. He took me round the American University and the hospital where he practised. I had the opportunity to observe a neck operation. At first it looked interesting but then I could not bear the sight. Thereafter Jamal insisted that I take part in a medical conference. The topic in the conference was »Hypertension«. It was really very interesting discussion. After the conference we had lunch with a gentleman, who was a member of the organisation and had spent quite some time in jail. Since it was a pleasant evening we all went to the beach and then walked up along the shore and back to the city. We had the dinner together. I thanked Jamal Musa and other friends and parted.

Next day I had a meeting with the newspaper. The journalist took a photograph of mine and asked me questions about my tour. He promised to hand me over a copy of the newspaper in which my story would be published. The same evening three German tourists came to the youth hostel. They told me that they had met two Indian fellows, who were hitch hiking, and met them in Jerusalem and again in Damascus. When they gave me some details of them, I knew at once that they were Ishaq and Nana. It was first time when I had a definite information that Ishaq and Nana were hitch hiking.

Return to Syria

Next morning I thanked all the friends and said farewell to the beautiful city of Beirut and started towards Tripoli. Hardly I had cycled up half the way to Tripoli when it started raining heavily. I got shelter in a house situated along the road. The rain did not seem to stop. Just as I was waiting a truck stopped in the neighbourhood and after some negotiation got a lift up to Tripoli.

I was carrying a letter addressed to a person in Tripoli. After some searching I could locate the house. The gentleman was very pleased to meet me. He arranged my stay in a hotel, where he asked me to hand him over my wet clothes so that they can be dry cleaned. I then wore fresh ones carrying with me. We had lunch together. Mr. Ammad, my host, had been asked to hold a lecture. This lecture was to be held at his residence, where more people were invited. After the lecture Mr. Ammad introduced me to his family. Thereafter we both went to the city, had some food in a restaurant and returned to the office. I insisted to sleep for the night in the office and to cancel the hotel reservation for that night. Next evening Mr. Ammad invited me to his residence and introduced me to his lovely sister and another friend of the family.

In the evening we visited the fort of Tripoli. The scenery far away from the top of the fort was very enchanting. This night I had to sleep in the residence of Mr. Ammad because the office was closed. Next day was the parting day. Though in the morning the weather seemed to be nice, but then it became cloudy and the rain started. Mr. Ammad and the whole family, specially the sister, insisted that I should travel by train to Aleppo. I thanked Mr. Ammad and his family for their hospitality. A taxi brought me first to the office where my baggage was deposited. After I had collected my bicycle and bags the same taxi then drove me to the railway station. After saying good bye to all the friends, who had come to see me off, I was again on the way to Aleppo. At first nobody in the compartment seemed to offer me a place nor anybody took interest to my person. A workman also travelling had with him a cutting from the newspaper about myself. This news rushed like fire in the compartment and very soon so many offers were extended for a seat that I and had difficulty to decide which seat I should take.

Aleppo

After about six hours journey I reached Aleppo. At the station I saw two scouts and asked them the address of Mr. Ummar. Unfortunately he was not at his residence, his servant was kind to allow me to keep my bags and the bicycle in the office of the organisation. In the meantime a group of young men had gathered around me, putting lot of questions about myself and about my objectives. I took out of my bag a cutting of the newspaper about me which was handed over to me before I left Beirut and showed them. They seemed to be satisfied and became more curious about my future plans.

During our conversation two persons entered the room, one of them was Elias. He asked me to be his guest. We were just getting ready to go when Mr. Ummer arrived. He was very pleased to meet me. He requested Elias if for the present I could stay in the same hotel with him. Later on another arrangement shall be made. Elias kept the bicycle at Mr. Ummars house and then with my bags we went together to the hotel where I was to stay for the next days. After I had occupied my room in the hotel I wished to have a bath after a long time. After the bath both Elias and myself went for a lunch to the city. After we returned Elias went straight to his room.

In the hotel lobby I met two girls who were talking to each other in English. I just flattering told them that they were the first female persons I heard speaking English. The girls were so flattered that they wouldn't allow me to go to my room. We sat down in the main hall and exchanged the views till midnight. I felt very tired and excused myself from my beautiful and charming company and went to bed. Hardly I was in bed when a page boy knocked on the door and asked me to leave the door open because the 2nd bed in the room would be occupied by a hotel guest.

In the morning Elias introduced me to a student, who should show me round. After the breakfast we visited the two big parks in the city, which were maintained very well. Thereafter I visited the Turkish consulate to get my visa confirmed. In the evening Elias opened to me that he had to go for an urgent job to Damascus and should return in three days and that I should remain in the hotel till he returned.

Next day I had dates with two newspapers and as usual gave information about my journey and handed them a photograph of mine. After that we visited the fort of Aleppo. In the evening while I was sitting in the main hall of the hotel, a young woman who later turned out to be a singer in a night club invited me and another gentleman also present in the hall to her room. She offered us some wine and cakes and wished us a happy Easter. Same evening when I came into the main hall she saw me and came forward and asked me in French whether I would like to visit the night club where she sings. At first I could not follow her but then she tried to make me understand with little singing. It was a tempting offer since I

السائح الهندي بالدراجة

يصل حلب في طريقه الى اوربا

وصل حلب السائح الهندي (اوم بريكاش فيرماني) قادما من الهند بالدراجة حيث غادرها في تشرين الاول ٩٥٤ الى بومباي ودلهي و كشمير و كراتشي وايران والعراق والاردن والقدس.

وطاف في دمشق وبيروت وطرابلس وحمص وحماة وحط رحاله مؤخرا بحلب التي اعجبته كثيرا وسر من مشاهدها وآثارها.

وقد سافر هذا السائح الى تركيا واليونان ويوغوسلافيا والنمسا وايطاليا وسويسرا والمانيا وفرنسا وبريطانيا.

وقد انهى (اوم بريكاش) دراسته في علوم الهندسة في بومباي وعزم على هذه الرحلة الشاقة بالدراجة.

وقد زار ادارة التربية واعجب بسير الاعمال فيها وصرح بانه سيكمل تمرينه في العلوم الهندسية بالمانيا.

Report in »Iraq Times«

had never been in a night club specially in an Arabian night club. I consented to the offer gladly.

She introduced herself as Jamila Samaan and asked me to get ready and accompany her. When I came out of my hotel room, I saw two ladies sitting in the drawing room. They requested me to sit down and offered me some coffee. Out of courtesy I took few sips of coffee, which was very bitter in taste. Jamila Samaan entered the room and we moved on to the night club. The night club was a very small under ground room, where the room was full of smoke and smell of beer around. Surprisingly western music was playing and a couple was on the dancing floor. The singer introduced me to the boss of the club and secured me a place near the counter, so that I was not disturbed and that I could see everything around me.

The singer Jamila Samaan

Hardly I had taken my seat when a group of ladies with curves of fine shapes and sizes appeared. They surveyed me from top to bottom and asked the singer who I was. She said something in Arabic and the girls left me alone. The western music started and a number of couples got up and started dancing. It seemed that the girls present in the night club were girls to incite the guests to drink and dance. One of them approached me as soon as the first dance was over. Jamila Samaan came to my rescue and told her to leave me in peace. She then bought some fruits and placed them in front of me I thanked her for the gesture and ate all the fruits.

After sometime the Arabian-night dancing started. A girl with quite voluminous curves started dancing, with hardly any clothes on. When I saw this the blood started creeping into my face and I lowered my eyes. When Jamila Samaan noticed this reaction of mine she gave a low laugh. I got accustomed to it after some time. After the dance Jamila Samaan came forward and started singing. Her voice was very enchanting. There was a great applause after she finished. The show went on up till about 2 o'clock in the morning. Since I felt tired I asked for leave and said good bye to Jamila Samaan and went to the hotel and went to sleep dreaming about what I had seen and heard.

In the morning Elias came back from Damascus we had tea together, then he went out to buy a newspaper. Hardly after a minute he came back running and told me that he had seen two Indians with rucksacks in the bazaar, we ran to the place but no sign of anybody. Disappointed we came back to the hotel, this was now the 2nd time that someone had seen both Nana and Ishaq. I went round the bazaar three to four times with the presumption least I meet them.

In the evening I went to see Mr. Ummar and thanked him for the hospitality and for the nice stay in Aleppo. Mr. Ummar handed over to me 30 Syrian Pounds, already converted in Turkish Liras by Elias for the further journey. My bicycle was brought to the hotel by the servant of Mr. Ummar. Next morning I was ready in my travelling dress. Elias brought me to the main road and embraced me and wished me all the best for the journey. I thanked him for the friendly hospitality and was on the road again.

I must have travelled about 30 kilometers when a small car overtook me at a glance I could see an army officer in the car. After further 20 kilometers when I reached the Syrian border, the same officer greeted me. After I handed over to him my passport for exit-entry, he told me that I had forgotten to report at Damascus to the police authorities, but then he was very helpful and telephoned to Damascus and got the visa-number intimated and entered in the passport. He then asked me if I would like to eat anything. Since I

Turkish border guards

was not feeling hungry I thanked the officer for the offer and moved on to the Turkish border.

Turkey

The custom authorities were very strict and asked me many questions before I could secure my entry stamp. The custom officer entered in my passport that I was carrying a bicycle. At first I did not care about this entry but at a later stage it did cause me lot of trouble. At the end they offered me some beer and Kebab to eat which I accepted in order not to offend them. I was about to leave when a journalist from Adana met me. He gave me his address in Adana and asked me to contact him when I reached there. We had a photograph together and then I proceeded towards Iskenderun.

The landscape all along up to Iskenderun was bright green. Without realising that I was cycling through a plane area without steep climbs I had covered about 40 kilometers and felt somehow tired. A Jeep overtook me. As a reflex I raised my hand and to my surprise he stopped and was kind to give me a lift for further10 kilometers. The jeep driver realising the situation asked me to travel further by bus. The money given to me by Elias in Aleppo was all spent, when I told him that I possessed travellers cheques only he stopped the bus and paid the fare up to Iskenderun for me. All the passengers in the bus were curious to know who I was. After they came to know about my tour they offered me food, drinks etc.

Iskenderun is a small port and beautiful. Unfortunately I could not find a place for overnight. Therefore I decided to proceed on and stay for the night at a small place on the way. After about 12 kilometers I came across a railway station called Payas a very small place, I went inside the station and requested the station master to allow me to sleep in the station for the night. The station master opened the waiting room for me. He was kind to offer me some food, I was really very tired and went to sleep. Next morning I thanked him and then continued my journey towards Adana.

A big climb came and I had to walk all the way. I do not know how long this steep climb was. After I had reached the top of the climb I made up my mind not to go on further like this way and travel further by bus. I waited at a bus stop and got a lift up to a small place called Ceyan then I took another bus to Adana. The passengers travelling in the bus were inquisitive about me. They asked me many questions, some of them believed that I was a rich man and was going round the world. A Turkish lawyer also travelling with us in the bus interpreted my story to others. A great appreciation was extended to my venture and no more questions were put.

After reaching Adana, I went in search of the journalist who had met me at the border. He was not in his office. His assistant could contact him at his residence by phone. He seemed to be very excited when he got the news. After his arrival he introduced me to the mayor of the town and a photograph with the mayor was made. Then he showed the parks of the city and told me that in the next days rains were expected. It would be better for me to travel further by bus to Ankara than by bicycle. Since I had already quite an experience with the rains in Syria I agreed to the proposal of the journalist. We both went to the transport office and booked a seat for me in the bus to Ankara. With the help of the journalist I could secure a bed in a hotel.

With the journalist in Adana

The journalist wished me a nice journey to Ankara and left. I then decided to rest for a while in the hotel and then went out for a walk towards the park. The evening was rather hot. People were sitting outside in the park. While I was sitting on a bench in the park a soldier came and started talking to me in English. During our conversation lot of people gathered around us. He worked as an interpreter for them. After this scene the soldier asked me if I was hungry, we both then went to a restaurant and had food together. The soldier would not allow me to pay my bill. I thanked him for the invitation and then came back to the hotel and went to bed.

In the morning I got up when I heard the shouting, which came from the bus station opposite to the hotel asking the passengers to take the bus for Ankara. I hurriedly took my breakfast, packed my bags and put the bags and bicycle on the bus. Unfortunately I forgot to remove the pump from the bicycle. I got a seat in the bus, a young man escorted his mother to the bus, she was going with us to Ankara to get treatment against cancer.

Ankara

It was a pleasant atmosphere in the bus. After about six hours journey we reached Ankara. It was raining when I got down at the bus station. The pump of the bicycle was missing. After I got down I had the idea to visit the embassy of India. At first it was difficult to find someone who could understand English. A person directed me to the said address by making a location sketch on a paper. In spite of this help I could not find the embassy. I was carrying an address of a person given to me in Aleppo. Luckily he was at home and I put my bags and the bicycle at his place. Then we together went out in search of a place for overnight. It was very difficult to locate the student hostel or the house of Y.M.C.A. Ultimately we went in search of a bed in a hotel. We tried in couple of hotels. Everywhere we would get the reply »yuk« which means no vacancy. As we were leaving a hotel a young woman followed us, she was also in search of a bed in a hotel. She accompanied us. Ultimately we found a hotel, where I could secure a bed for myself but she was not accepted. I was tired and went to sleep.

Next morning Ahmet, the name of the young man at whose place I had kept my bags and bicycle, came with a friend to the hotel. We all together went to the embassy of India. To my great surprise I saw Nana sitting there. We met each other after about two months, when I asked him about Ishaq he mentioned that Ishaq was hitch hiking separately and therefore had not yet arrived in Ankara. Since it was Sunday nothing could be arranged at the embassy.

Since Nana also had no accommodation we all together decided to go in search for a possibility to stay. We tried at two school hostels. To our bad luck either the director of the hostel was not present or there was no place vacant. Then Ahmet got an idea that since I had covered all the distance by bicycle why should not we try to get a room in the stadium. We now proceeded towards the stadium. There was a football match going on between a team of the Turkish Army Vs Air force. With the assistance of Ahmet we approached the director of the stadium. He heard the story and promised to help us but asked us to wait till the match was over.

After the match the director welcomed us and gave us some money and then sent us to the person in charge of the stadium. A room was put to our disposal. We were glad for this gesture. Nana also was glad for this possibility and wished to stay with me. I accompanied Ahmet to his house and brought my bags and bicycle to the stadium.

The same evening while leaving the stadium we saw big posters of the Indian Film »Awara« which means »Vagabond«. I just remembered the song in the film and started humming the tune of the song when a person came from behind and caught my shoulders and asked me whether I had seen the film. He then invited us to see the film and after the film for a dinner. We accepted the invitation. When we reached the cinema the film was running. We were told that it was sold out. He bought the tickets in the black market and so we saw the film „Awara. After the film we had food together.

Next day we went to the embassy of India, to our surprise Ishaq also had arrived the previous night from south of Turkey. He was suffering from cold and could hardly speak. Therefore he avoided to talk and made himself understand by signs. We wished to meet the ambassador and were shown in by the first secretary to the ambassador, who first inquired about our journey and was pleased to meet us and asked what he could do for us. We requested him to give us reference letters addressed to the ambassadors of Greece, Yugoslavia, Italy and Austria. He gladly gave us the said letters. Now all three of us were together again and stayed together in the stadium. The next five days were spent in securing the said visas.

One of these evenings Nana opened to us that he intends to travel further by train to Istanbul and then to Austria and further on to Backnang in Germany where he had to meet somebody from the company AEG-Telefunken. The next morning he left for Istanbul. We saw him off at the railway station.

The following evening Ishaq and myself went to the post office to get some stamps. It was closing time. The woman behind the counter asked me whether I was from India and then she told me that she saw the Indian film »Awara« for five times and every time there were lots of tears. She then closed the door of the post office and requested me to write down the text of the song in the film which I gladly did. For this obligation she did not charge me for the stamps I needed. This scenery was being observed by a Turkish architect, who was also present in the post office. He invited us both for a sight seeing tour of Ankara the next day. Together we visited the old city of Ankara and then the monument of Kamal Ataturk at a hill, where in the evening the mausoleum is lighted by strong light beams. The Turkish architect then invited us for a big feed because it was their national holiday. Many Turkish dishes were served. For this marvellous day we thanked our host and came back to the stadium.

In the evening Ishaq asked me whether we could travel further together. At first I thought to travel further by bicycle alone, just then

Ishaq reminded me of the good old long friendship and confessed that he would better travel with me than with Nana. He did not give any further reasons. At this moment I wished to ask him about his reasons for his refusal to travel with me as was announced by him back in Karachi. I do not know what came over me I could not ask him about it and consented to his request with the thought that in a company one enjoys more and agreed to hitch hike further together with Ishaq than to travel further by bicycle.

Since my bicycle was entered in my passport I visited the custom authorities in Ankara and asked them whether I could sell my bicycle. At first they refused but then a custom officer came forward and asked me if I would sell my bicycle to him. I had no alternative but to agree to the proposal and sold the bicycle to the custom officer.

The following day after thanking the person in charge of the stadium we were again on the road to Istanbul. The first lift we got was by an air force truck for about six kilometres. Before leaving the truck the driver told us to try for further lifts at the petrol station. We followed his advice and went towards the service station. A truck full of flour gave us a lift up to Izmit. In Izmit a group of people gathered around us when they saw us both with Australian hats and were quite inquisitive about who we were. After finding out about our venture they invited us for a feed in the restaurant and also paid for the overnight in the hotel. The Indian Film »Awara« was running in the local cinema, they arranged such that we had a free entrance to see the film.

Europe

Istanbul

NEXT MORNING WE WERE AGAIN ON THE ROAD. First we had short lifts with a fire brigade car and a bus. Ultimately we got lifts in two different trucks going towards Istanbul. It being Ramadan (the fasting month of Muslims), the driver gave a part of his food to us. About 20 kilometers to Istanbul one tyre of the truck got punctured. The driver first tried to repair the tyre but after about two hours gave up the idea and fixed the reserve tyre of small size, this reserve tyre left us in lurch after about 2 kilometers to Istanbul. We marched the remaining distance and reached the sea. We had a plan to stay for the night in the youth hostel. We asked somebody on the road for the address which we were carrying. We reached the address, but to our surprise we found out that another club was situated at the said address. At the reception when the ladies saw us with the wide brim hats they laughed but then helped us to the right address.

The secretary, a Jew, gave us a very cold reception, he was very talkative but no effective help. He then said if we were willing to pay we could remain in Y.M.C.A. At first we felt a bit relieved but when we heard the amount he demanded we left the place and went in search of a cheap hotel accommodation. After a long searching we found a place. There was a strong smell around but we had no other choice. In the morning we left as urgently as possible and went to the university, where I had the address of Mr. Mithat, given to me by one of the students in Damascus. When we met Mr. Mithat, he was very pleased to meet us and asked us to stay with him. We had with us our sleeping bags and therefore no inconveniences were to be observed by Mr. Mithat. He introduced us to two further Syrian students, Mr. Shauki and Mr. Alexander.

Next day a visit to the historical part of Istanbul was planned, where Mr. Shwaki agreed to show us round. We met him at the university premises and from there we started for the tour. First of all we visited the Mosque of Sultan Ahmed or so called the Blue Mosque having six minarets and a circular dome. The oriental architecture work with blue coloured embedded marble pieces is really worth seeing. Then we visited Hagia Sofia. Here one can really see the different ruling periods. First the Christian era and at the same place the Muslim period. During our visit we met a lame man, who could speak many languages, also Hindustani: He related to us his story that he had met Indian soldiers during the 2nd world war and had learned Hindustani from them. He explained to us about the water cistern, which was built to provide drinking water to the whole city. There were about 336 columns of water, now it served as an ancient historical monument. Thereafter we visited the Totkapi-Serail Museum, the ancient china clay work of different Dynasties and different periods. Also the glass china clay of other countries. Then we visited the sultan palace and the tulip gardens.

In the evening we had a meeting date with Miss Gözen, a pen friend of Ishaq. I had to buy a map of Europe and other necessities. During this shopping time Alexander and myself somehow got separated from Ishaq. We were of the impression that he might have gone ahead to be in time for the date so we took an underground train and reached the docks where we had to take the boat. When we knocked at the apartment door Miss Gözen appeared in the door. She was astonished to see Alexander with me. I introduced him to her. We sat down and were just doing conversation when Ishaq arrived. Thereafter we had a long discussion about marriage, women etc. This conversation extended to subjects like religions in

India etc. It was rather late in the evening when we came back to our hosts house. We had our evening meal with Mr. Mithat and then went to sleep soon dreaming about the meeting with Miss Gözen.

The following day we had planned to go for a picnic to one of the islands on the Bosporus. Miss Gözen wanted to accompany us but then changed her mind. Mr. Shawki and Alexander decided to accompany us to the islands. We took a ship to one of the islands. While we were at the lower deck of the ship, we heard the music with clapping and dancing going on. When they saw us some of them came forward and asked whether we were from India and then asked us whether we know about the Indian film »Awara". When they came to know that I knew the text and also could sing the song in that film, they all together forced me to sit down at a higher platform and the accordion player started with the music and I sang the song. They were fascinated about it. By this time we had reached our destination. We all got down and went round the island and after sometime we went to a restaurant and had some snacks. During the lunch we were discussing whether we should visit the next island or go back. Being late in the afternoon Alexander proposed to join the group with the music. We followed his proposal. Soon we were enjoying, dancing singing when one of the girls came forward and told me that she loved me. Another girl said the same words to Ishaq. The boy friends of both the girls wished to initiate a fight with us, probably out of jealousy, but somehow the other friends came forward and asked them to quiet down. The girl at my side, named Birsen, was a romantic type. She would not budge an inch from my side and was telling me all the time she did not love her boyfriend any more and that I was her life. I was rather confused, she would take my hand and try to take me away from the others. Then she asked me for a dance, she would not dance with anybody. Her boyfriend was so disgusted from the situation that he insisted that I should take her along. Others present there were enjoying the situation. Then we decided to have photographs together: Ishaq with one of the girls dancing with him and Birsen the girl dancing with me.

A short romance on the ship on Bosporus

By this time the ship had reached the port. Just as we were parting from the group, Birsen came forward and asked me to take her along. I was in an awkward position since everybody was watching us. I then told her that I shall take her after I had returned from Europe and then kissed her hand and left. Now we decided to visit Miss Gözen. Mr. Mithat accompanied us to her house because he was fascinated by her photograph and was curious to meet her. Miss Gözen met us at the door step and then requested us to come that night so that we can visit some of the interesting places at night.

Mr. Mithat decided to leave us since he was fasting. Ishaq and myself decided to remain in Kodikoy and see around. First we went to the post office where Ishaq mailed few letters home. Then we visited the market. Late in the evening we went to the residence of Miss Gözen. Her parents were waiting for us. We chatted for a while and then drove towards the highest place from where we could see the Bosporus and all the city of Istanbul. Next we visited the place from where the whole city is supplied with water. Miss Gözen showed us the place where she went for swimming in summer. We had dinner together in a hotel. We thanked our host for the grand evening and returned to the house.

This was our last evening in Istanbul. Next day was the labour day and the first day of spring in Turkey. We got up early in the morning, packed our bags. We had a heavy breakfast together. The parting was short and sweet but sorrowful. Once again we were on the road toward Greece. First we took a ship from Üsküdar to Biotu, said good bye to Asia and entered Europe. We came to the outskirts of the city and waited near the highway. All the people gathered around us as usual our outlooks with wide brim hats fascinated them. However, after the people came to know that we were Indians, the first question was whether we knew the song in the Indian film »Awara«. I sang for them. During this singing many five Lire coins fell in my hat. Then we were invited for a drink in a restaurant. By this time it was late afternoon and we could not get a lift.

Ultimately we decided to walk along the road and stop cars and trucks passing by. A municipal truck stopped and gave us a lift for 5 kilometers. We had travelled about 20 kilometers, when a bus stopped. We got into it and the bus conductor demanded money. We were arguing with him for the price, but then all the passengers in the bus shouted »Let them come in!«. When we sat down the conductor refused to take any money from us. We made quite a number of friends in the bus, they offered us coffee and sandwiches. We reached the border city of Edirne.

We left our bags and sleeping bags at the bus agency and walked round the city. Ishaq had to buy a film. When we were leaving the shop, a man who could speak English came forward and inquired about us. After knowing our identity he declared to show us round the city. He guided us to the Mosque of Saleem. We agreed to climb 210 stair steps to get on top of the turret of the Mosque. Since we both were used to walking, we did not feel the climb, but our host, a teacher of the physical training, was grasping for air. The Mosque is one of the biggest with beautiful painting work including china-clay tiles of different colours and designs. After the visit we asked the man whether we could be permitted to sleep for the night in the school. After returning to the bus agency he tried to contact the director of the school but had no luck. The man then approached one of the owners of a hotel and explained to him the situation. The hotel owner agreed to accommodate us free of charge under the condition that we gave his son some lessons in English. We agreed to this deal. Then we went back to the bus agency and brought our bags etc. to the hotel.

In the evening, when we went out to see around, we met two German students travelling by a Volkswagen bus. We asked them if they could give us a lift up to Thessaloniki the next day. At first they agreed to take one of us, however, suggested to decide after inquiring their accompanying friends. We went back to the hotel and gave the son of the hotel owner a lesson in English.

Later in the evening as arranged with the German students we went to the place where the Volkswagen bus was parked and to our surprise noted that two further American students were accompanying. The German students were ready to give us a lift but the American students would not agree to it.

Next morning, after the breakfast we took our Rucksacks and sleeping bags and were again on the road. This morning there was hardly any traffic. We got a short lift by a horse cart, which brought us to the Turkish custom and passport authorities. We got the necessary stamps in our passports. Since there was no traffic we decided to march on to the Greece border, however not realising that the border was quite some distance. After two hours walk in the hot sun sweating and tired we reached the Greece border. After the custom formalities and the necessary stamps in our passports we continued our march.

Greece

Just as we were walking, a car passed by. We tried to stop it but the driver refused to give us a lift. After some time we saw a group of women and girls sitting together in the sun, knitting and chatting. We took a photograph with them and then moved on again. We rested a bit in a restaurant, had a modest meal and then pushed on again. As we were moving, somebody passing by suggested to us that we should take a short cut to reach the first city after entering the Greece border. We followed the advice and the result was, that we had to walk 20 kilometers to reach Orestias - the first big city after the border. We were very tired, as such we had been walking since morning with resting intervals. We walked round the city, when the chief of the boy scouts met us. Seeing our outfit with wide brim hats he thought that we were also boy scouts. He asked us to be his guests and arranged for our stay. He invited us to a restaurant, where we had a grand feed with greek dishes.

In the evening when the life began on the main streets of the city, we were introduced by the chief of the boy scouts to quite a number of people, who put us lot of interesting questions about ourselves and about our venture. Late in the evening he opened to us that the Queen Frederike of Greece planned to visit Orestias the next day and that it was a good opportunity to see and meet the Queen. We gladly accepted the invitation.

It was warm but since we were tired we went to sleep soon. Next morning after the breakfast we went out in the city which was being decorated for the visit of the Queen. Till late afternoon we remained in the city and changed all the Turkish Lire into Greek Drachmas. Thereafter we went back to the hotel and got into our national dress, which we were carrying with us for special occasions. Just when we were having our lunch, a friend of George came into the restaurant and seemed to be impressed to see us in our national dresses and proposed to pay the bill for the food and drinks. After the meals when we came on the street where people were waiting for the Queen, a teacher saw us, came forward and told us that he had been in Sudan, where he had met quite a number of Indians and promised to introduce us to the Queen.

A girl by the name of Margaret surveyed Ishaq from top to bottom and then passed the remark in her language: »Don't you know the Queen

Conversation with the queen Frederieke

is visiting us and you are wearing your Pyjamas«. Everybody laughed. Ishaq was very impressed by her remarks and of course looks. At last the Queen arrived, we were allowed to stand near the honourable representatives of the city. When the Queen approached, the people showered flowers along the road and clapped their hands in her honour. Since nobody was there to introduce us we took the initiative and went forward and introduced ourselves to the Queen and related in short about our venture. We mentioned that last day we had walked all the way from the Greece border to Orestias. She was pleased and impressed to hear that and then - to encourage us - remarked »well you could depend upon your own legs«. Then we had photographs together. Ishaq asked her for an autograph in his passport. She then told us that Mrs. Indira Gandhi and herself are close friends and if we had the chance to meet her we should extend her best wishes to her. Then she wished us good luck for our journey.

We then went back to the hotel changed our clothes and got ready to take the bus to Alexandropolis. Unfortunately the last bus had already left before we could reach the bus station. We then decided to stay for overnight in the railway station. At first the station master was against it but then agreed to our request. We left our bags etc. at the station masters office and went out.

The people had gathered round the park. Our conversation with the queen was quite impressing for young boys and girls in the town and they showed a keen interest to meet and talk to us. We gladly exchanged our views. After an hour we left towards the bazaar to take some food. On the way we met a girl name Evan. Ishaq was very impressed about her beauty. We went to the railway station and brought the sari (Indian lady dress) which he was carrying with him and ask Evan to wear it and helped her into it. Then he took a photograph of her. She did look charming in the Indian Sari. Ishaq told her many times that he liked her, thereupon she thanked him every time he said that to her. She requested Ishaq to send her a copy of the photograph. Ishaq promised to do so.

Visit of queen Frederieke in Orestias

George, one of the young man, who had been accompanying us all the time, then declared that he was intending to visit the house of the prostitute on the outskirts of the town. He asked us weather we were interested to join him. At first we refused to do it but then out of curiosity we decided to have a short visit of it. We accompanied George and his friends to the said house.

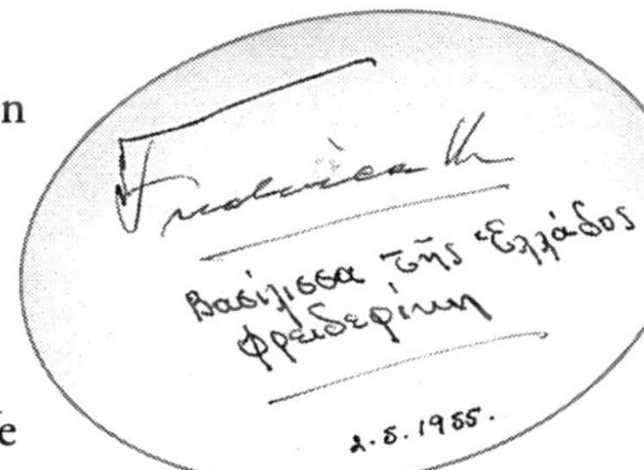

After some waiting a woman with voluminous shape of curves appeared. George and his friends who knew her from her constant visits were quite free with her. Some of them were clapping on her buttocks other were holding her breasts. We stood there flabbergasted and left the place hurriedly. During our visit through Greece we were told that a high percentage of the males do visit regularly the prostitute houses.

We came back to the railway station and since we had to get the early bus the next morning we prepared ourselves to go to sleep. In the morning we got up, packed our bags, thanked the station master and proceeded to the bus station. On the way there we had a hurried breakfast and were once again on the road. After about four hours journey we reached Alexendropolis.

After reaching we first decided to have a swim in the sea, but after finding no suitable place for it started walking on the main road to be picked by a vehicle towards Kavala. We walked about five kilometers and sat in a garden with an eye on the road so that when any vehicle would approach we shall get up. We were not lucky to get a lift. Hungry as we were, we decided to eat something and went to the next hotel but could not find anything suitable and walked towards the next one. Just then a truck passed our way we tried to get a lift. Fortunately it stopped and took us to the next two towns. After the first town the driver took quite a time to go further for the next one, because he had to load a horse and two donkeys, which was a time-robbing job, therefore we spent the night in the truck only.

Next morning we thanked the driver and were again on the road. We walked through the city and had a short ride in a horse cart of a farmer up to the farm. After reaching there we again went to the main road and sat down beside the road. After a long time an empty truck gave us a ride up to Kavala. After reaching there we started walking alongside of the road. Hungry as we were we went to buy the bread and cheese separately to save some money. But when I put my hand in the pocket to find out that there was not much change in Greek Currency. We both returned from the shop. A man who noticed this gesture asked us why we did not buy the bread and cheese. We explained to him the situation. He bought the bread and cheese and gave these to us. We had just started to eat when a jeep passed and stopped on our request. He asked us about our destination. On hearing that it was Thessaloniki he asked us to get into the jeep and said that he was also travelling to Thessaloniki. We were glad that the driver accepted to take us in the jeep. After arriving in Thessaloniki he dropped us on our request at the office of the boy-scouts.

Thessaloniki

The office was closed so we decided to have a swim in the sea. First Ishaq got into the water but the water smelled bad at this place so we decided to go little further. Ishaq was the first to go into the water. After he had finished I got ready to have a swim. As I dived into the water I lost my underwear, the spectators gathered around us and found the situation funny and would urge me to come out. Ultimately I had to come out of the water naked. We changed our clothes and went back to the office of the boy-scouts.

The house keeper asked us to leave our baggage there and come back in the afternoon. A young man who was present with us all the time accompanied us to a park and the white town. We spent this time to visit an exhibition of biblical books. Since we were tired we sat down on a bench in the park. After about two hours rest we came back to the office of boy-scouts. Mr. Makaridis apologised not being able to help us because he had sometimes back accommodated some scouts without the permission of the police, since then it is restricted to accommodate any foreigners.

We were then directed to the Y.M.C.A, where Mr. Castor in charge of the association was pleased to help us out and allowed us to stay as along as we wished, however we had to accommodate ourselves in a room which had chairs and tables only. Since we were used to the hard way of life we made the best out of the situation. We kept our bags etc. there and then accompanied the young man, who had guided us to the association. In the evening when we came back to the association we had the chance to meet a good number of young boys and girls. They would not let us go to rest. One of the boy could play on a piano and so an improvised music concert took place. It being late we both went to sleep with a promise to meet them again next day.

Next morning Mr. Michel, a member of the association invited us for the breakfast to his house. This invitation was extended up to lunch. During this period we were discussing about Indian Culture and about Cyprus. Thereafter his romantic father joined us and we had the lunch together. During the lunch his father said that he liked and loved Soraya, the queen of Iran and that he has written to her too and was expecting a reply. In the evening we could visit few monuments in Thessaloniki. Thereafter we visited the university, where we had the opportunity to meet many male and female students.

It was a full moon night and soon the romantic verses of romantic poetry were recited. It was pretty late when we realised that we should hurry up before the Y.M.C.A closed its doors. But then an invitation from the students was extended to spend the night at their residence. We gladly accepted the invitation and the result was that we all went mighty late to bed. Next morning we all met at the Y.M.C.A premises.

We both then decided to proceed on to Athen and packed our bags and said farewell to our friends and were again on our way to Athen. First we tried to get a lift on a ship. The harbour authorities were ready to give us a lift if we would wait for two days. Since we did not have more time to our disposal we came to the main road leading to Larissa. A truck gladly gave us a lift up to Larissa, the driver was a jolly fellow. After arriving in Larissa we took a photograph with them. The driver arranged for another truck going to Athen. We reached Athen without any incidence.

Athen

We spent the night after arrival with the scouts, however later on we found out that we could spend as many days as possible at the student hostel. During this period we visited a number of ancient monuments like Acropolis, Small Acropolis in classic style, the old Palace, now being used as parliament house and the museums. Then we decided to make a trip to Peloponnesos, specially to visit Mykene, Epidauros and Olympia, Travelling there included short lifts per bullock carts, full of olives and with trucks. We reached Mykene late in the evening. We started looking for a place to stay for the night when we reached the ruins where the gold treasure of Agamemnon was found. A small hotel in the vicinity of this monument was the topic of discussion between Ishaq and myself. Our conversation was heard by a French grand old lady. She came forward and explained that she was an artist and would love to participate in the expenses for the stay in the hotel. At first we hesitated but then she insisted that we should be her guests. We thanked for the generous invitation and took a room in the hotel.

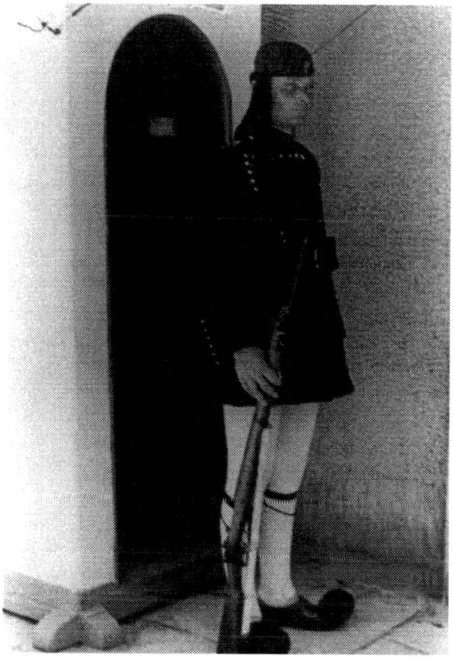

Palace guard in Athens

She being an expert gave us a short review of the monument of Agamemnon. Mykene is situated about 25 kilometers south of Korinth and was destroyed 1100 before Christ. In 1874-76 Schlieman excavated the city walls, where within the walls 6 graves with gold work, Colony Palace outer court yard, Lion Gate and gold treasure were found.

After visiting the ancient monuments we decided to hitch hike further towards Epidauros. In Epidauros we visited an ancient Greek theatre in very good shape with 55 seat rows and where in 1821/22 the national assembly was held. Our next visit lead us to Olympia. The travelling there

Grave of Agamemnon in Mykene

Ancient Greek theatre in Epidauros

was full of adventure, we had to travel by bullock carts, old trucks etc. Here we visited old archaeological museums, Temple of Hera, Old treasury houses and the Olympic stadium. After visiting these places, we returned back to Athen.

In Athen we had an opportunity to take part in an excursion with the boy-scouts. In fact we could not take part in all the activities of the scouts. We all had a swim in the sea. Here we met a group of nurses who had come out for a picnic, they tried to teach us the love language in greek and as a compensation we gave them lesson in swimming. All the same we had jolly good time together. We stayed one more day with the scouts to take rest before we wished to start again to Thessaloniki and then towards Yugoslavia. But the evening was full of surprise: Our hosts gave a grand party, where lot of wine was drunk and we had the greek dancing. Due to this party we started late in the morning. It was hard for us to find the main road, but with the help of the police we could get to the main road. First we got a lift in a truck for 30 kilometers. Then we could get another lift in a truck, where the driver later on decided to proceed after 3.0 p.m. Ishaq was not keeping well, he had many drinks at the party, therefore he went to sleep under a tree.

After a long waiting we got a lift in truck. We both being tired slept in the truck. After an hour we reached Larissa. The truck driver asked us to wait there and promised to arrange for further lift by another truck towards Thessaloniki. To pass the time we went round the city and after some time returned to the office of the truck owner. He asked us to wait till the evening. We thought we could at least try to get a lift by another truck and moved towards the main road, but before we moved we requested the owner of the truck that he should kindly ask the drivers to look for us, if we could not succeed to get a lift. We walked about two kilometers out of the town and then sat down in a restaurant, which served as a border toll house, where a policeman kept the record of the incoming and outgoing traffic. Here every truck had to stop before proceeding further. We tried to get a lift in one of the trucks, but they had place for one person only, therefore we decided to travel separately up to Thessaloniki.

As soon as the next truck arrived I asked Ishaq to proceed first and I shall follow him in the next truck. I was very hungry and proceeded towards the restaurant and wanted to buy some bread and cheese but then noticed that I had only dollar notes in my pocket and was just intending to go away when a person standing in the restaurant noticed this situation and asked to bring bread and cheese for me. In no time the bread and the cheese vanished into the stomach. Just when I left the restaurant a truck stopped, the driver told me that he shall be travelling 14 kilometers that day and proceed further the next day. Since it was boring to wait I decided to take the lift. After reaching the destination I left the driver and proceeded towards the city. As soon as the people saw my outlook they gathered round me. From the spectators a person came forward and started talking to me in English. When he heard my story in short he was very pleased and then invited me to be his guest. We went together to his house, which he said was destroyed by the Italians and has been reconstructed by himself. He introduced me to his wife. She asked me whether I was hungry and offered some food and drinks. After I had some food the man and myself went out and landed into a coffee house. After about two hours when we returned to the house a grand dinner was waiting for us. We had the dinner together. This was now the second time that I had the opportunity to be a guest of a Greek family. After the dinner Vasilias, the son guided me back to the place where the truck was parked. Tired as I was I opened my sleeping bag and went to sleep on the grass.

Early next morning we were up again and moving on the road. The driver was a quiet fellow and his assistant just the opposite. He borrowed my mouth organ and played variety of music on it. In the afternoon we reached Thessaloniki. After reaching there I went straight to the Y.M.C.A. and changed my clothes. In the meantime Ishaq also returned and we both went out to meet the old friends. George was very pleased to meet us again. Ishaq decided to remain with the group, which decided for singing, dancing and of course drinking. I spent the night with the sympathetic family, where I was accepted as a part of the family. Next morning Ishaq and myself went round in search of some possibilities to get to the border of Yugoslavia. All the trucks going towards the border refused to give us a lift. Everybody we met advised us to take a bus to the border and thereafter travel by train, because there were strict controls by the police authorities. Since we were used to getting lifts we thought to try and if it did not work up we shall travel by train. In the afternoon we took a bus to the border of Greece. When we reached the border we were sent back with the arguments that hitch-hiking is not allowed in Yugoslavia. We were asked to go to the next railway station. Since there was no train due at that time, we spent the night in the waiting room of the station.

Yugoslavia

Next morning we bought a ticket up to Skopje and took the next train going to Belgrade and got down in Skopje with a hope to be able to hitch hike further. After leaving the railway station we started walking on the road to get to the main city. We could notice many curious eyes watching us and a light whispering going round among the spectators. Out of curiosity a young man followed us and after sometime approached and asked us about our destination. We told him that we wanted to see the city and then wish to hitch-hike further to Belgrade. He advised us to go by the train because hitch-hiking involves permission and control by the authorities. We requested the young man to show us a place where we could eat something. He guided us to a restaurant. The restaurant manager refused to serve any food without the coupons. While we were discussing about the possibilities a man entered the restaurant and inquired about the situation. After knowing the problem he left the scene and after sometime returned with a number of coupons and gave it to the young man so that he could buy food for us. We had a decent meal and thanked both the men and left the restaurant and headed straight back to the railway station.

Belgrade

We bought a ticket up to Belgrade and waited for the next train scheduled in an hours time. The train arrived. To our surprise we discovered that seats in the compartment were simple benches without the backs. We could secure seats in the compartment, though at first sight it looked fully occupied. In the train we met a Yugoslavian lady also travelling to Belgrade. We were lucky to converse with her in a cocktail mix of English and French. After she came to know about our venture she appeared to be fascinated about it and promised to be helpful in Belgrade. Our conversation with her was of general nature as such she was careful not to discuss with us any political or other subjects which would cause her difficulties.

After reaching our destination we helped her with her baggage out of the compartment. She was pleased by this for her very unusual gesture. She asked us about the possibilities of our stay in Belgrade. After she knew that we intended to stay in the student hostel she asked us to accompany her to her residence and promised to help us further. We gladly accepted the offer and accompanied her to her residence. At the residence she introduced us to her husband and the two lovely daughters. The couple expressed their inability to accommodate us as their guests, because otherwise they shall have regressive difficulties with the authorities. We remained with the family for few hours and had some hot drinks together. Some time later they asked their daughters to accompany us to the student hostel. We all four travelled by a tram to the student boarding house. Both the girls accompanying us were helpful explaining the warden of the boarding house about our situation. The warden checked thoroughly our identities and then agreed to allot us a room in the boarding house situated few blocks further on. Both the girls excused themselves for not accompanying us further and said good bye to us and left.

During our stay in the student hostel we were the guests of nine students and of course met many more students studying in different faculties and had the opportunity to discuss about their system of social communism, which had not followed the guidelines given by Russian communist party. During our discussion every student took precaution not to criticise the system least they may have to suffer some regressions. We had the opportunity to join lectures on English and History. The following days we visited some museums together with the Co. students. For the last evening of our stay the students organised a party where everybody contributed for drinks and different dishes. After the food we all danced with the music from the radio until the dawn set in.

It was bright daylight when we decided to have a walk in the adjoining garden to the hostel. After some walk everybody laid down in the grass to have a short sleep. After some hours we got up and went back to the hostel premises. Two of the students gave us the address of their friends in Zagreb and asked us to contact them on arrival. Late afternoon we decided to proceed on and after parting from the students took the train to (**Agram in Croatian language named Zagreb**). With the constant rhythm of the running train we felt very tired and drowsy and started dreaming about the previous night. We got up when a sound from the station loudspeaker announced the arrival of the train in Zagreb.

In Zagreb we were overwhelmed by the friendliness of the people. Maybe there is some difference between the people in Croatia and Serbia. Our host a young man received us with his fiancée. They arranged our stay with their family. Next day we accompanied them to the university and had the opportunity to attend the English lectures. A group of students joined them. It was a great fun when the assistant professor noted our presence. After the lecture a group of students joined us and we all went together to visit different places. In the evening a grand dinner was arranged with a large group of friends from the neighbourhood and Co. students from the university of Zagreb. This was once again a pleasant experience in Yugoslavia.

Our next destination was Ljubljana. Since we had the possibility to travel by train only, we decided to leave the country the next day by train to Trieste. Our aim to meet people and get an insight of the culture and the regional worth seeing places was partially fulfilled taking in view of the existing system of the Government and institutions. We were, however, fortunate to have had the opportunity to meet quite a number of students who irrespective of the centrally ruled government-system discussed with us about their system and how they made best out of it.

At the end of our stay our friends accompanied us to the railway station to see us off. We said goodbye to our friends and farewell to Yugoslavia and were once again on the way to the next station of our journey.

Italy

Three days before the end of month May we entered Italy. In Trieste we went straight to the youth hostel, which was situated on a hill where a rack railway carried all the passengers to their destination. In the evening the city looked very enchanting with the harbour lights. We remained there for a day to get hold of some Italian currency. In the youth hostel we met many students from different nations, who were travelling round Europe by hitch hiking. This was encouraging for us for further travelling.

Next day we went to the outskirts of the city for a lift to Venice. We got a straight lift up to the city of Venice and then went in search of a youth hostel (in Italian language »Ostello«). Though it was the high season for the tourists, we were lucky to get accommodation in a youth hostel situated not far away from the centre of the city of Venice. We kept our bags at the youth hostel and visited the enchanting city of Venice. First day we visited the famous Marcus place and the Marcus church with five dooms and its 99 Meter high bell tower. Afterwards we went to see the Doge palace and Canal Grande with the famous Rialto Bridge. Next day we tried to cross as many bridges as possible (Venice has about 400 Bridges) and 150 water-channels and few antique-pillars. Also we could bargain for a reduced price for a ride in a gondola. In the youth hostel we had the opportunity to meet young students from USA and Germany.

On first June we left the enchanting city of Venice and after crossing the narrow lanes took a trolley bus up to the outskirts of the city. As soon as we got down the trolley bus we noticed a little further on that all the passing traffic was stopped to pay a toll before going further, we now saw the chance to ask the stopping cars for a lift. Since Ishaq and myself had already agreed about our route to Rome we agreed to follow the route also separately in case we could not hitch hike together. I was successful to get a lift up to 30 kilometers, whereas Ishaq could manage to get a straight lift up to 89 kilometers.

After two further lifts I met Ishaq in Bologna and as usual we went straight to the Ostello and secured each a bed for the night. In the youth hostel we met a young married couple. They had decided to spend their honey moon by hitch hiking and spending their stays in the youth hostels.

Ishaq was mad about the daughter of the Ostello-Mama and flattered her by singing loving songs during most of the period we remained there. Here we met an Arab chap who mentioned that he had travelled quite a distance by bicycle and was now hitch hiking. He would do anything to get hold of money. He was in the youth hostel for the last fortnight and hadn't paid for his bed and food. Youth hostel mama would have been pleased to get rid of him. Ishaq spent the evening in the company of the daughter of the youth hostel Mama and I spent the evening in the company of Germans in the youth hostel. In the hostel we met George, who was very much interested in art and promised to show us round the next day.

Next day was the national holiday in Italy, it was the republic day. We noticed that all the soldiers were gathered on the streets. We were anxiously waiting for George to join us. After long waiting he came and proposed that we should go round by bicycles. Gladly we agreed to the proposal. Ishaq wanted that his present love, the daughter of the Ostello-Mama should accompany us. Obviously he had to get the permission of the Mama and was successful to convince her and the daughter could accompany us. Ishaq would not move away from the side of the girl, they looked like a very romantic couple going hand in hand laughing, joking etc.

After returning to the hostel we requested the daughter if she could stitch for us on a piece of cloth carrying the words »INDIA« by sewing machine, so that it would help us to get lifts on the way. In fact the people thought that because of our Australian hats we were south Africans or from Spain or south Italians. The young girl gladly stitched signs for us. Cycling up after a long time was quite tiring for us so we remained in bed late in the morning. Ishaq proposed that we visit the laboratory of Marconi, but later on were informed that the firm no longer exists. Mama was enthusiastic about us and gave us coffee and something to eat. Ishaq was all the time in a romantic mood and sat hand in hand with the young girl.

Next day was our parting day. We thanked mama, our host and said good bye to her and the young girl. Not to confuse the Mama and specially the girl Ishaq gave a kiss on the forehead of the girl and kissed the mama as the French people do. We came on the road with our signs on our chests. Ishaq was little sad on this day. We could notice the courageous responses from the drivers of the passing cars. After 30 minutes a car first passed us and then stopped suddenly after 100 meters and then reversed the car and stopped beside us and inquired whether we were really Indians. After he saw our passports he asked us to get into the car. He explained that he is a manufacturer of motor cycles and was successful but he was not successful with his private life. He would like to get a divorce but being a catholic could not take such step. He left us at the outskirts of Florence from where we took a tram to the center of the city and reached the youth hostel. After reaching there we met young tourists from Australia, South Africa, USA and England.

We were offered a free pass to visit all the museums and galleries of the city of Florence after they came to know that we were from India. We thankfully accepted this offer and visited the biggest gallery »Uffizi Gallery« with all the paintings of the 13th and 14th century and the Uffizi Palace. We wanted to visit the birth house of the famous poet Dante, who was born in Florence, but then decided to meet students at the university. The exchange of views with the students was very interesting.

In the afternoon we decided to hitch hike further to Pisa. We came out to the main roads towards Pisa. Since it was not possible that we both, Ishaq and myself could get a lift together we agreed to travel alone to meet again in Pisa. Ishaq got a direct lift to Pisa, whereas I could get a lift for 10 kilometers only. The driver left me on the road.

Since it was getting dark I decided to travel further in the morning. Now I went in search for a night shelter. I saw a farm a little further along the roadside and on my request the farmer allowed me to sleep in the barn and gave me some bread and wine to drink. I thanked the farm owner the next morning and was again on the road and managed to get a lift up to **Pisa.**

I met Ishaq at the youth hostel. We remained there for two days. We visited the leaning tower of Pisa and the cathedral. After two days we left for Rome our next destination. We knew that we may not be able to get a lift together, in that case we decided to meet after reaching our destination and that the youth hostel was the meeting place. Ishaq got a lift, whereas I was still waiting for one. It seemed that I shall be having a tough time for getting a lift because two girls were also waiting for a lift but I was fortunate to get a straight lift to **Rome.**

Rome

Ishaq and myself had agreed to meet at the new youth hostel but after reaching **Rome** I noticed that I had misplaced the address of the new youth hostel. Now I tried to get to the old address of the youth hostel, I met an English girl and asked her about the said address. She accompanied me in the tram and we came to the youth hostel. The warden of the youth hostel opened to me that the youth hostel was totally booked out and that I had very less chances. The English girl accompanying me then told the warden of the youth hostel about my venture in short. This naturally opened the heart of the warden. He then asked me to hand him over my youth hostel card. The warden then remarked that my card was going to be invalid in two days and had to be renewed. However, he allotted me a place for the night. I kept my bags. and joined other tourists in the big hall. Here I met a group of Yugoslavians.

6th June 1955

I could not contact Ishaq and went with the Yugoslavians to see the museums, because they were allowed to visit the museums free of charge. After visiting the museums I took leave from the group and went to the Indian embassy for getting my passport extended. Here I met the ambassador who was minister in the Indian embassy in Damascus and had told me that he is due to go to Rome as ambassador of India. He was very pleased to meet me. He then asked the counsel officer to renew my passport. I got it renewed gratis. I thanked the ambassador and went to the city. Here I cashed a travelling cheque near St. Peters and then returend to the youth hostel. In the evening I joined the Yugoslavian group and we exchanged our sight seeing experiences.

7th June 1955

Early morning when I got up, the two Germans, two Canadians and the Yugoslavian group had already left. **I slowly got dressed and with a horrible shock realised that all my money (Travelling cheques, Dollars, Lire) was not in the pocket.** I at once brought the situation to the wardens notice. He remained non impressed and said he can not help me I should report the matter to the police. At this moment I wished I had not lost the address of the new youth hostel and Ishaq had been with me. I went to the police station and had to wait till a constable arrived, who spoke English and could make the report. I told the policeman about the loss. Fortunately I had the numbers of the travelling cheques issued by Thomas & Cook in Bombay. The Policeman made the report and handed over to me a copy of it so that I could report the loss to the agents of Thomas & Cook in Rome.

During this report at the police station an Englishman who was also waiting to report was a witness of the situation and after hearing my story felt very sorry about the whole situation. He took 100 Lire out of his pocket and handed over to me as his contribution. He asked me about my destination. On hearing that we intended to go over to England explained to me that he was a manufacturer of cloth specially cord stuffs in Manchester and employed quite a number of Indians. He promised to give me a job in his firm when I would have reached England. I thanked him for his kind offer.

Out of anxiety I asked him why he was at the police station. He mentioned that he was on a camping holiday outside Rome with his family and was visiting the historical monuments and museums in Rome and when they returned to their camping place the tent and all the utensils were stolen and now he was reporting it to the police authorities. He said that he shall have obviously to make other arrangements than camping. I tried to console him by saying that he was in a more tragic and tough position than I was since he was in Rome with his family.

After leaving the police station I visited the tourist office of the Thomas & Cook and informed them about the mishap in the youth hostel. They apologised not being able to help me at once. They stated that the stolen travelling cheques shall be refunded only after the tourist season is over. The maximum time shall be at least three months. The same evening I was successful in contacting Ishaq and told him about the mishap. At first he was surprised that it happened to me but then he consoled me by saying well we shall shorten our journey and try to reach Germany as soon as possible.

Our plans were to travel further to Naples and visit the historical monuments of Pompeii.

We had to give up these plans. We decided to return to **Pisa** and then further on to Milan and over Austria (Innsbruck) to Germany. Though next day it was a big catholic holiday, yet we were successful in getting lifts to return to Pisa. At the youth hostel a French girl asked us whether she could accompany us to visit the cathedral and the leaning tower of Pisa. We had no objection. First we visited the cathedral and then the leaning tower, here the French girl posed as if she was supporting the leaning tower Ishaq took quite a number of photographs in this posture of the tower. We came back to the youth hostel. After our lunch we decided to move further towards Geneva. The French girl gave me a farewell kiss on my mouth, the lips were smeared, she came forward and removed the lipstick from my lips. She joined us to the outskirts of the town and again parted from us as the French people do.

First we were picked up in an open motor-cycle -Wagon and travelled about 20 kilometers. Then we were picked by the same English gentleman, who three days back had given us a lift in his jaguar to Rome and brought us straight to the youth hostel in Genoua. We thanked the gentleman and wished to see him again.

In Genoua we remained for a day and then proceeded further towards Milan. As soon as we came to main road to Milan, we were lucky to get a straight lift to Milan. The gentleman brought us straight to the youth hostel. We decided to remain in Milan for few days and try to get a job to earn some money. I went to visit an Italian friend who had visited India touring by motor cycle and had asked us to visit him when we come to Milan. Unfortunately our friend himself was not in Milan, his mother was very hospitable to us she promised to help us secure a temporary job. We had a recommendation letter and this way tried to find a job with Lambretta, Magneti Marille but without any success.

Without wasting any further time we decided to move out the next morning. We took a bus and came to the outskirts of Milan. At first we got a short lift up to a small village, from there we got another lift where the gentleman hearing our story stopped on the way and took us to a small restaurant and asked us to drink wine, we could not refuse and took quite a number of glasses of wine. He then left us at the main highway to Bolzano. We could manage to reach Verona and then tried to get a further lift and were successful in getting one by a truck carrying fruits.

As soon as he left us a group of girls, probably street girls saw us and invited us. We realising the situation moved away from that place hurriedly. Since we could not succeed to get a further lift we first decided to spend the night in a church but then it was too far away from the main road so we came again to the main road and tried to find a house along the main road. Luckily a person in the house allowed us to sleep in the barn of the house, provided we handed him over our passports. We had no alternative and gladly accepted the offer. It was really nice to spend the night in a barn full of hay. In the morning we got some bread and milk for the breakfast and some peaches. We thanked the farmer and were again on the main road.

5th June 1955

As soon as we came to the main road we got a lift to the next town and then further small lifts to **Bolzano.** Here we could hear that people were talking with another in German. We were the object of attraction. We bought some food and then sat down along the roadside for a lift. It was after a long time that we got a lift for 20 kilometers. The man was a reporter of a German newspaper in Italy. He advised us to wait at a straight stretch along the road and avoid slopes. He left us at such a stretch along the road. It was a grand surprise when a Volkswagen stopped next to us. The person driving it was the same person who was also present at the police station in Rome, he asked us whether we wished to go to Germany. With great relief we confessed that Germany was our next destination. He asked us to get into the car and we moved on. He told us that after the war he was working for the American companies. He added that, a big number of companies of American soldiers are stationed in Garmisch-Partenkirchen. At the present time he was working for a German newspaper in Munich.

Austria

We reached the Italian Border, got an exit stamp in our passports and a little further got an entry stamp by the Austrian border police-authorities. After some travelling we were in the Alps, high mountains all around. All the time the Volkswagen, famous for its robust construction was leaving back the steep climbs. All of a sudden down below we could see the enchanting lights of the city of Innsbruck. The car rolled on along the curves down to the city of Innsbruck. We crossed the city without stopping anywhere. Again we were in the hills. After some time we came out into the open area, a little further on was the border of Austria. We got an exit stamp in our passports and drove on.

Germany (West Germany)

A little further on was the border of Germany. We got the entry stamps in our passports and moved on further towards the city of Mittenwald, the first border city in Germany. At about 10 p.m. we reached the youth hostel. It being summer time, a large group of young people were in the youth hostel from different parts of Germany. The young people greeted us both. The »house father« as they call it in Germany for the »warden« of the youth hostel refused to accommodate us because the youth hostel was totally full. With the assistance of the journalist we tried to explain the warden our situation that we were coming all the way from India and that it would not be possible for us to arrange anything anywhere at such a late time in the evening. Ultimately the house father found a solution, he brought cots and placed them in the kitchen. We were of course pleased to have this asylum for the night. We thanked the journalist our host and tired as we were went to sleep as soon as we were in the bed.

At the youth hostel in Mittenwald

Next morning when we got up the house father demanded one Deutsche Mark for the lodging. But when I explained to him about the mishap at the youth hostel in Rome he showed understanding and agreed to give us free lodging and food if we would help in the kitchen and do the cleaning etc.

We gladly accepted the offer. We were asked to peel potatoes. While peeling the potatoes among a group of other young people a girl remaking asked the house father, why I had such a dark brown colour. The house father joking remarked »he does not wash himself«. At first I did not understand but then someone out of the group explained the joke to me. The first job was to peel the potatoes and then cleaning the canteen.

Next morning we went to the barber shop to get a hair cut. Ishaq, who was fond of passing compliments took the chance to practice it at the barber shop. As we waited at the barber shop, an old couple entered the shop. Ishaq was sitting next to the old woman, he held her hand and said that her eyes were blue as the clear sky and her eyes were as the moving cloud in the sky her husband hearing this laughed and said bluntly that her eyes were black and turning to Ishaq asked him whether he intended to court his wife. Ishaq was so shocked from these comments, that he gave up the idea at all. After a haircut we returned to the youth hostel. In the evening we decided to move on to Munich the next day and to try to get some work there.

We thanked the house father for the help and moved towards the motorway entrance. We got a straight lift to Munich. It being Sunday all the shops were closed. We decided to stay in Munich at least two days and went straight to the youth hostel.

We visited the museums, Nymphenburg Palace and the park, the mayors house with the campanile having Bavarian figures which move around with a chime of a melody, the Maximianeum, German Museum, the national theatre, St. Michael cathedral (as motive in the Town flag or signet), last not least the last evening the Hof-Brewery, where we had the chance to drink a glass of beer. After the beer we were tired and hurried to reach the youth hostel and soon went to sleep.

The following day we took a bus to the outskirts of the city and then to the motorway entrance towards Stuttgart. To our surprise we noticed a little further on a group of girls which were also hitch hiking. A car stopped at once to pick up these girls but we had no chance. We tried to get a lift by the American cars but they would hardly take any notice of us. After a long waiting we got a lift for 30 kilometers. Then a small car with a trade mark „Gogomobile" gave us a lift up to Stuttgart. It was pretty dark when we reached Stuttgart. Since it was raining we took a bus to the youth Hostel, though it was late but we could manage to secure the accommodation for the night.

Next morning we met a small group of girls, who invited us to join them to Ulm, but our next destination was in the opposite direction towards Bonn. We were late to move out of the youth hostel. After reaching the outskirts of Stuttgart we had to walk about 4 kilometers before we came to the motorway. Unfortunately it was not the right exit. A police car stopped and after asking about our destination told us that it was not the right exit and asked us to go to the next one. The next exit was about 6 kilometers further on, we walked through the woods alongside of the motorway. We noticed a couple of middle age little further on. But after some nearing saw that they were courting we just went on and came to the said exit. We waited there for a long time but without any success. Just as we were thinking to go back to the city, a car stopped and brought us to the next service station and dropped us there, saying here we had better chances of being picked up than at the exit we were waiting.

At the service station a truck driver, who had already two girls beside his seat agreed to give us a lift, provided we agreed to sit at the open back. We had no choice but to agree to the proposal. After some distance both the girls got down and we both took seats in the front. The truck driver was on his way to Essen to deliver the truck. We wanted to get down at the exit »Siegburg, Bonn« to get to Bonn. That day the motorway was under repair and therefore the police was guiding the traffic at many places. It being dark outside we could not make out where we were. Upon inquiring the driver replied that we are nearing Cologne and had already passed the exit leading to Bonn. It was about 10 p.m. we requested the driver to drop us at the next exit.

We were now about 30 kilometers from Bonn, it was dark everywhere, we did not know which direction we should proceed. Thirsty as we were we started walking towards the direction of light far away. We were at the outskirts of the city and saw the wagons on the railway-tracks so we proceeded towards the control tower and went up and requested the person in charge for some water to drink. At the first sight the man in charge and his colleague were surprised but after our explanation offered us water to drink. We thanked them and then proceeded towards the city. Here we entered a café, when the people saw us with our wide brim hats and our outfit with the bags we became the center of curiosity. We asked for some coffee and bread. After eating some dry bread and coffee we left the coffee house.

Now we had to search for a place where we could sleep for the night. Obviously we had to take care that we are not far away from the motorway, so that we could get a lift in the morning back to Bonn. After some searching we found a place where there were many trees around. We were tired, opened our sleeping bags and crawled into them.

Early in the morning, when it was slowly getting bright, we got up little stiff and surveyed our surrounding. To our surprise we found ourselves in a garden of a house. We hurriedly got out of our sleeping bags, rolled the bags and moved on before we were discovered by the owner of the house and marched back to the motorway. A travelling agent gave us a lift up to Siegburg. From there we got another lift up to Bonn. After reaching Bonn we went straight to the university youth hostel, kept our bags etc., washed ourselves, dressed up and in the afternoon visited the embassy of India.

Before starting on our tour we had written to the Indian embassy in Bonn for assistance in securing work for specialising in the field of telecommunication with well known firms like Siemens or Telefunken in Germany. The reply from the embassy was that it could be arranged when we are in the country itself. On arrival we showed the letter to the ambassador. He directed us to the cultural department in the embassy where we were told that the selection and the nomination of the candidates takes place in India only and that they could not help us to this effect.

During our meeting with the ambassador I disclosed to the ambassador about the mishap in the youth hostel in Rome and showed him the report of the police authorities in Rome. Mr. Majumdar, the ambassador at that time opened to me that officially he sees no possibility to help me out but if anybody in the embassy would like to help me he shall have no objection.

Disappointed we both left the embassy and went back to the youth hostel of the university in Bonn. During the meals in the Mensa, (canteen for the students) we met two Indian students who after coming to know our story promised to help us and after the meals guided us to the student association office and introduced us explaining the diversity of our situation. The person responsible in the student association offered us a temporary job in Bad Godesberg, where a flower exhibition had just ended and all the stalls had to be dismantled. We gladly accepted the offer.

The day was warm, we both took off our shirts and began to work. It was a hard work removing and carrying away wooden girders. We worked for 16 hours. At the end of the hard work we received DM 50,- each. A grand feeling for the first self earned money. With this money we could go on for a week. Our plan was to get any job to earn money and brush up the German language to get a better chance for specialising.

During our stay in the youth hostel we came to know an Indian student who after hearing about our story introduced us to a German lady, with a very pleasant affability and a tall stature of approx. 2 Meters. She had taken over the responsibility to promote the exchange of German-Indian-Culture and according to our information she had been helping many Indian students studying in Bonn. After hearing our story she asked us whether we were prepared to accept any job. On hearing a positive reply from us, she asked us to sit down, picked up the telephone and called somebody. The person at the other end of the line heard the story and straightaway asked her »can they play Hockey« Since at home back I was in the college hockey team the reply was »yes«. The person at the end of the telephone asked us to meet him the next evening at a hockey field situated next to the river Rhine. Also we were asked to visit him at the firm called »Rheinische Schmirgel Werke«, where we should get the possibility to work.

The whole situation looked very promising. It was now my part to do my best so that it should lead to some success for both of us. The whole evening and the next day some tension was to be noted in our behaviour, as such many thoughts went through our minds. Next evening we went to the said hockey field and met the gentleman on the phone. To our surprise the gentleman introduced himself as the president of the »Bonner Hockey and Tennis-Club« and also as the owner of the »Rheinische Schmirgel Werke«. On arrival at the hockey field I was handed over a hockey stick and asked to play with the players on the field. I took off my shoes and barefooted joined the game. All the players and the president were very impressed about my play-technique. The president then consulted the team captain about the possibility of my integration in the team.

Next morning we went to the said firm. Since our job was of temporary nature we were asked to work in the packing of sand paper grinders before they were sent further to the freight department. In this department there were three male workers, Ishaq, myself and the manager of the department surrounded by 14 women worker. We were taken up on hourly basis salary of DM 1,30 with 48 hours per week.(i.e. Monday till Friday 9.00 hours per day and three hours on Saturday). We were lucky to find a room with a family in Beuel, a city on the other side of the river Rhine, where also the said concern was situated. The grand mother of the family was also our mama.

After about two weeks the owner of the firm called me in his office and asked me whether I was interested to play regularly in the first team as centre forward and also was prepared to take up the training of the young girls and boys playing in the junior teams, at least once a week. If I agreed to the proposal I shall be allowed to remain absent from work for that day with payment. I agreed to the proposal with a request that I should be allowed an additional half day for studying at the university of Bonn to fresh up my German and French language. The owner agreed to this arrangement.

Beside this arrangement practically every Sunday we had matches against other regional teams of the league to achieve the top ranking. Ishaq

Hockey training in Bonn

couldn't join me because he was not confronted with hockey sports back home, though he had taken part in many other sports like boating, boxing and weight lifting etc. He remained in Bonn for the next three weeks and then left for Bielefeld to attend a student summer camp and then to Interlaken in Switzerland to attend an international summer camp. I remained in Bonn because I had a commitment for training the junior hockey teams and also because I was not keeping well.

My gums were effected, probably because we used to eat milk products only. It was not an adequate nourishment as we were used to back in India. The women co-workers showed sympathy with my situation and brought along pudding etc. so that I could eat at least something. Under this situation I had to consult a doctor for treatment. The medical doctor after examining my gums gave me calcium injections and advised me to change my eating habits and eat also ham and meat, if necessary after cooking, to compensate the necessary requirement of the body. I agreed to the diagnose of the expert and followed his advise and this way recovered in the following five weeks.

The next task was to search for another accommodation because our old landlady required the room for her family. Temporarily I shifted to the university hostel and tried whatsoever time was available, to find another accommodation, but was not successful. Mr. Martin, a specialist in the same firm invited me to his house. His wife, also a refugee from East Prussia heard my story and showed sympathy with my situation and offered to stay with them for the time being till I had found an appropriate accommodation. This way I became a part of the family of Mr.

Martin and was welcome as an adopted uncle for their children, a boy and a girl.

9th August 1955

I was in the best mood for work. At about 11.00 a.m. Mrs. Martin came to the firm and handed over to me a letter from Thos. & Cooks. They had asked me to collect the money stolen in Rome. In the evening a colleague of mine was helpful and we drove on his motorcycle to the branch ofThos. & Cooks in Bonn and collected the money and then went with some friends for swimming. After the swim I requested my friend if we could drive to the embassy of India to collect a letter from back home. We collected the letter and came back home. When I opened the letter, the joyous day turned into a tragic day in my life. In this letter my brothers and sister had tried to disclose to me the death of our father who after a long illness died on first August. The last letter of my father reached me on 10th June 1955, in which he did not even mention about his illness, least I would be worried.

Next day I decided not to go to work and wrote a letter home. Since I was very sad, Mrs. Martin asked me whether I would like to accompany her with both the children and visit her mother living in Bonn. I accepted the offer and visited her mother. Her mother tried to console me. With gratitude for the mother I left them to meet other Indian students at the university of Bonn.

During our stay in Germany we had the opportunity to visit the cities of Hamburg, Berlin, Cologne, Düsseldorf, Stuttgart etc., of course by hitch hiking. In all these cities we could note the bombed buildings, where most of them showed burned signs. Also we could note that the rebuilding work was done by day and night to achieve more living room than was available to accommodate the local people and the refugees from East Prussia, Silesia etc. Also I remember the visit of German chancellor Mr. Konrad Adenauer to Russia, where he had talks with top Russian delegation.

These talks resulted to the diplomatic relations between Germany and Russia. On return Russia promised to release all the German prisoners of war detained in Russia. In October 1955 we could see touching scenes in the cinema news and television when the returning prisoners were received by their relatives and friends. During my work in the coming months I came to know quite a number of Germans, who were prisoners of war in Russia, Great Britain, France and USA. They would relate about their experiences as soldiers and as prisoners of war in the said countries. Those were very sad narration and I wished deep from my heart that there should be no wars at all at any place on earth.

After three months period I had to get my visa extended till end of 1957. After three months of study at the university of Bonn, I disclosed to the owner of the firm that I had studied Electrical Engineering and would like to do something else than packing the sand grinding papers. Hearing this he disclosed to me that he was very pleased with my efforts as regard the training of the junior teams was concerned. He offered me the job of an assistant to the works electrician to gain more experience in the technical installation technique including a loan of DM 2,60 per hour. Since I had no better offer at that time I agreed to the proposal.

In April 1957 I visited the Industrial Fair in Hanover and visited the stalls of the firms AEG, Siemens and Rhode & Schwarz. An engineer of the Siemens concern showed interest for my qualification. He asked me whether I was interested in the installation and maintenance of telephone equipment with a possibility to work later on for their representatives in India. I was very pleased to get such an offer and agreed to the proposal. He asked me to come to Bielefeld, where he was assistant engineer and shall arrange everything when I am there. After returning to Bonn I disclosed the owner of the concern about the offer. At first he did not seem to be happy but then said well it is a chance for me to go forward and if the offer is genuine I should accept the offer and try my luck. At the time of leaving a reference letter was handed over to me certifying that I was a good hockey player and trainer and worker. I said good bye to the family Martin and all the friends in the hockey-club and left for Bielefeld.

I wrote a letter to Ishaq and informed him about the new situation. Since Ishaq had been to Bielefeld he gave me the address of a family in Bethel, a part of Bielefeld. I visited the family Linnemann and they gladly accommodated me as their guest until I could find an appropriate accommodation. The following day I visited the subsidiary of the Siemens concern and tried to contact the said engineer. To my great surprise I was informed that the said engineer had himself left for South Africa. The Siemens-branch-Manager, after hearing my story was impressed and wished to help me. He invited me for a meal and informed himself about my qualifications and experience so far. At this stage I thought it to be wise not to mention to anyone how I had travelled to Germany. After the meals he telephoned with a small firm responsible for electrical installations and inquired whether they could offer me a job. I got an offer to do the installation work for Adler works, producing sewing machines and gladly accepted the offer with a grand salary of DM 120,- a week. During this work I came to know few students who were doing diverse jobs on the building site to earn some money during their holidays.

After I had this job I thought to do some sports and - having good experiences in the hockey sport - tried to find out a club where I could play hockey and this way extend the circle of friends. I read in the local newspaper that a hockey match would take place on the coming Sunday. I went to the said address and asked a player about the possibility to play hockey. The player after knowing my nationality introduced me to the captain of the team. After I explained him in short about my experience in Bonn, he handed over to me his hockey stick and asked me to play. I was in my normal dress, but accepted this offer and took out my shoes and barefooted started playing. The captain and other players were quite impressed about my playing style and asked me whether I was interested to play in the team. I must confess that I was expecting such a question. I gladly accepted the offer and so far my finances allowed I bought a hockey stick and the shoes so that I need not had to play bare footed. The club members arranged the club dress for me.

The work at the building site was not very pleasant because it was very draughty during the work. After about four weeks I started thinking of quitting the job and intended to search for another one. And in case I was not successful, I intended to leave Bielefeld and go over to Berlin, where Nana was working with the concern AEG. When I mentioned about my intention to a club player he informed the captain of the Hockey Club. Luckily the captain knew personally the manager of the subsidiary of the concern Telefonbau & Normalzeit GmbH, which manufactured and installed the communication equipment like telephone, master and slave clocks, time registering equipment, etc. I agreed to accept a job with the said firm, if I was given a chance.

A week later the technical Manager of the concern interviewed me and at the basis of my qualifications offered me a job as a helping assistant to the installation expert. I regarded this offer as a chance and accepted it and joined the work. During my further activities I came to know that the main works are in Frankfurt on the Main and that they exported communication equipment to India, specially for Indian state parliaments.

In October 1956 I wrote a letter to the export manager of the concern in Frankfurt on the Main with the question, whether I had a chance to work for their subsidiary in India. The reply was very positive. I was asked to come to Frankfurt for a personal interview. As a consequence of this interview I was given a chance to gain further experiences with all their product systems. I remained in Bielefeld for one year. At the beginning it was difficult to be accepted by the Westfalian people. It is true when they say that it is difficult to win the heart of a Westfalian, but once they accept you they are friends for life. In Bielefeld I had an opportunity to do some promotion work about India. I was asked to hold a lecture before a forum of fifty persons of different nationalities over »cast-system in India«. I prepared the lecture very thoroughly and had the feeling that it had a great acceptance. In order to come in contact with the German culture I was told that the classical literature by Goethe and Schiller and the classical music compositions by Beethoven, Mozart and Schubert are worth studying. I tried to study the literature for the short time available to me.

One evening I decided to go to the theatre to see an opera, but was not allowed in because I was not dressed up accordingly. For this reason I decided to save money and get an appropriate suit made and this way visited few musical presentations in the theatre. I was slowly getting settled, when one day the subsidiary manager opened to me that there was an urgent installation work to be done at the world-exposition in Brussels, specially for the German-Pavilion and the Air line Sabena. He asked me if I was interested to go over to Brussels.

At first I was pleased to get such an offer but was somewhat hesitant because it meant leaving the new friends made in the hockey club and otherwise, however, considering the chances of gaining more experience and for the future prospective, I accepted the offer.

The first step was to get the necessary visa. The Consul General of Belgium in Cologne sanctioned a visa for three months only. It was really sad to part from so many friends. In November 1957 when I left for Brussels by train, quite a number of friends came to the railway station to see me off.

The management of the subsidiary in Brussels had arranged a room for me and further two young Germans from Berlin with a family in the Interlaaken area, not far away from the Palace of Belgium Royal Family. For the first two nights I had to stay in a hotel and then shifted over to the guest room with the family. Our host belonged to the Flamish group, whereas his wife belonged to the Walloon group. Our host had experienced bad treatment during the occupation by the German army in the 2nd World War and was therefore not quite pleased to accommodate the two young Germans in his house. The father in law of the host, who was also occupying a part of the house was very pleased to meet me and after knowing that I had the knowledge of the Persian language and had visited Iran, opened to me that he had been ambassador to Iran and showed to me his copy of the »Rubayate Kheyam« and recited few verses out of it.

During the period of my stay in Belgium I tried to find out the possibilities of doing some sport. Just by chance I came to know that the crew of the Sabena Airlines were active and took part in team sports like Hockey and Badminton. The player in the teams came from different nations, a cosmopolitan team. I was welcome to play in the Hockey and also in the Badminton team. This way I got the opportunity to see more of the country. We had matches in Ostende, Antwerp and Bruges. At the exhibition ground I could notice daily the progress in construction of the »Atomium«, a significant symbol of the Exposition. I remained in Brussels until the end of March 1958.

According to the arrangement with the German concern Telefonbau und Normalzeit GmbH, I returned to the main offices and research laboratories situated in Frankfurt to gain further insight of their products range and testing systems.

In the beginning it was rather difficult to get any accommodation in Frankfurt because there was not enough room available and all around the city of Frankfurt buildings destroyed by bombing was apparent, however with the assistance of the personnel department of the firm, I could secure a furnished room not far away from the concern. My room was simply furnished with a cabinet and a sideboard on which was placed a large broad bowl in which was placed a large mug full of water for washing etc. As such most of the houses did not have facilities for taking a shower or bath. Majority of the habitants would use on weekends the public washing facilities.

For the next six months I was sent to the main production works. Here I gained further experience with regard to the assembly and the final control of Telecommunication equipment before it was supplied further for installation. One day the head of the department visited the works and by this opportunity told me that he has been informed by the director of the export department that due to shortage of foreign currency reserves Indian Government had withdrawn their orders for the present and therefore my chances to work for their agents in India had to be postponed for the present.

But since I had gained good experiences with their products by installation, testing and approval for the last three years they were interested to engage me further for the design and development work in their labs. Consequently they asked me to consider about this offer so that necessary arrangements could be done. I regarded this offer as a grand chance to gain further experiences and agreed to the proposal. After a probation time of three months I got the confirmation of my job with a salary on monthly basis.

This was a grand challenge for me to show that I could work hard so that I would be accepted by the German colleagues. However, I did not mention to anybody about my venture from India to Germany, with a motto »they should judge and accept me by my work and efforts and not what I had done in the past«. I thought that I should disclose about my venture when I am older and have settled down. The new job meant a raise in the salary, this meant that I could now afford a better accommodation than I was living in at present. I started searching for a comfortable accommodation. At first I decided to insert an advertisement in the local newspaper. Just then I read on the information board at the personnel division that a furnished room was to rent. With the assistance of the personnel department I was successful to rent this room. My Landlady came as a refugee from Silicia (now Polish territory) and was working in the same firm.

My daily life became a routine, going to work daily and in the evenings studying the technical books and documents. At this stage I had no chance to meet people, except on Saturdays and Sundays. After few weeks had passed, I felt that I should do some sports and this way as in the past come to know some people. In the local newspaper I read about a hockey match on Sunday. After inquiring I reached the said club, where the hockey match was going on. On the field I asked my neighbour about the name of the club and about the possibility to play. He gave me his visiting card and asked me to come on the coming Tuesday to the stadium.

I had the opportunity to demonstrate my play technique and was welcome to play in the team. Saturdays and Sundays were reserved for matches against other teams of the league.

I noticed that mostly all the members of the team were accompanied by their family members and young members by their girl friends, when we had matches against other teams of the league. At these occasions I used to feel lonesome and cherished an internal desire to set a basis for a family. In India it is a tradition that the parents search for an adequate match for the boy. After both the boy and the girl have seen each other and have agreed, they get married. Now since the parents were not there I had to decide for myself alone. I believe that I must have during my conversation with the landlady disclosed to her that if I meet a girl, who is genuine with her intentions to get married and accepts me as I am I shall ask her to marry me.

One evening my landlady showed to me some photographs of an excursion with her colleagues which was organised by the concern for the promotion of good relations among the colleagues. In this photograph I noticed a colleague of hers with sunglasses and just passed a remark that her colleague was good- looking. With this remark my landlady proposed that she would gladly introduce us when I was in the office.

Every morning I used to drive by my scooter to join the duty. It was just luck that one day my scooter refused to start. I had no choice than to ask my landlady whether I could get a lift in their car to join the duty. Since my landlady also worked in the same concern she consented to my request. After reaching there she asked me if I would like to be introduced to the good looking colleague of hers on the photograph.

At first I hesitated to be introduced at the concern premises but then out of curiosity followed her to her office. My landlady introduced me to her and after a shake hands and hallo we both went to our offices. But Elfriede Wengenroth, so was her name, had made an impression on me. So there followed quite a number of rendezvous after this first short meeting. During these rendezvous we came to know each other well.

After a few months Elfriede and I got engaged and started making plans together to ge married.

The first challenge was to get the necessary permission from the registry office. At first it seemed easy to get a licence for marriage but then it turned out that lot of formalities regarding documents were necessary. I could not provide my birth certificate because my birthplace was totally destroyed by earthquake in 1935. To prove that this statement of mine was genuine I made a photocopy of the page in the dictionary where all the places of earthquakes are documented and presented it to the lawyer and under oath made the statement that my birthday is identical as given in my passport. This document was accepted by the registry office. The next step was to secure a marriage licence, for which I had to apply to the high court. After about three months time it was sanctioned. I had to pay a months salary as charges for it.

Our first visit to the registry office was also eventful. The officer in charge demanded three times the charges for registration as was usual for a normal German couple. On reminding the officer about this discrepancy, I was told that they charged such an amount from a foreigner. Thereafter he told Elfriede, my fiancée, that it was his duty to bring to her notice that her fiancé according to Indian constitution was allowed to marry four times. At first I myself was surprised by this statement and tried to explain the officer that the example of Indian constitution he held in his hand was issued in 1929 and that India was a colony at that time. In the present edition of the constitution published in 1959 states clearly that only Muslims are allowed to marry four times. But the officer refused to accept my arguments and asked Elfriede to sign the statement that she was brought this to her notice. I made a sign of resignation and left the situation to her to decide for herself.

I was so annoyed with this treatment and asked the officer whether it was compulsory to marry where you had registered. The officer mentioned that it was not compulsory. Thereupon I told the officer that we shall get married in Frankfurt and not in the present registry office. The officer defending explained that the present office is a palace, where

Napoleon had spent the night. I retorted that we shall get married in the Frankfurt registry office, which is also famous because many kings and emperors were crowned in that building. So did we: exactly on the same date after one year when we had met for the first time Elfriede and myself got married.

In the following nine years the family increased to five persons. In 1960 our son Arun was born, in1964 our daughter Kiran and in 1968 our daughter Indra. It was the beginning of a new phase of life which was a challenge for both of us to see that the family had all the necessary provisions of life.

Arun studied chemical processing technology, Kiran did her doctor's degree in nutrition science and Indra specialized in industrial marketing and sales promotion.

In 1962 together with my wife Elfriede and Ramesh, a classmate of mine who lives in England and is married to Marian, an Englishwoman, we made another adventure tour to India by Volkswagen car. The route of the journey was over Austria, Yugoslavia, Bulgaria, Turkey, Persia, Pakistan to India. We reached our destination in 14 days. Well, this is a new story and experience.

I close my story now with the hope to continue it, if possible, complete with the family at a later stage.